Phyllis Thompson

EACH TO HER POST

Six women of the China Inland Mission

Amelia Hudson Broomhall
Jennie Hudson Taylor
Margaret King
Jessie Gregg
Jessie McDonald
Lilian Hamer

HODDER AND STOUGHTON

and

THE OVERSEAS MISSIONARY FELLOWSHIP

British Library Cataloguing in Publication Data

Thompson, Phyllis
  Each To Her Post: six women of the China Inland Mission.
  1. China Inland Mission—History
  2. Missionaries—China—Biography
  3. Missionaries, Women
  I. Title
  266ˈ.023ˈ410510922   BV3427

ISBN 0 340 26933 2

Hodder and Stoughton Editorial Office: 47 Bedford Square, London WC1B 3DP

EACH TO HER POST

CONTENTS

ACKNOWLEDGMENTS

I am very grateful to all those who have contributed comments and advice in the compilation of these biographical sketches, especially to the Overseas Missionary Fellowship for permission freely given to quote from their books and publications, and to Dr. Eldon Whipple and Mrs. Margaret McDonald for invaluable notes and information about Dr. Jessie McDonald.

AUTHOR'S NOTE

When James Hudson Taylor founded the China Inland Mission in 1865 he broke fresh ground in two areas. One was in the sphere of finance, as he launched out with his band of followers making no appeals for money, but bringing all practical needs to God in prayer, believing that 'God's work, done in God's way, would never lack God's supplies.' That this principle worked has been proved time and time again, not only in the history of the Mission he founded, but in that of many other missionary societies founded since that time.

The area of innovation was that of personnel. In 1865 it was unheard of for a missionary society to send single women to the interior of a country such as China for pioneer work, and was a move which came in for widespread and severe criticism at the time. It demanded a high quality of courage and spiritual conviction for young women from sheltered Victorian homes to embark on such an enterprise, blazing a trail into the unknown for others to follow. Jennie Faulding, later to become the second wife of James Hudson Taylor, was one of them.

Margaret King and Jessie Gregg joined the Mission about thirty years later, and went to cities where work had already been established. Their distinctive contribution was in the realm of pioneer evangelism among the women of China, one among country women, the other among those from the better educated classes. They were outstanding revivalists in their day.

Jessie McDonald was a pioneer in another field: that of medicine. She was the first fully qualified woman surgeon in the C.I.M. which she joined just before the First World War, when women surgeons were a rarity anywhere. At the height of the Second World War she opened a hospital in the remote province of Yunnan. It was here, exactly eighty years after the Mission was founded, that Lilian Hamer, the indomitable little mill girl from Lancashire, joined the staff. The story of her service and sacrifice to reach the Lisu spans the period during which the China Inland Mission became the Overseas Missionary Fellowship.

The sixth woman in this little book of biographical sketches comes into a different category. Hudson Taylor's sister Amelia has been rather a shadowy background figure in the annals of the Mission he brought into being, yet she had a most significant bearing on it. She was her brother's closest confidante for years, and from the beginning to the end of his life she was woven into its warp and woof. Let us draw back the curtain of time, then, and meet a thirteen-year-old Victorian schoolgirl, complete with corkscrew curls, a demure expression, ankle-length skirts and well starched pinafore, named Amelia . . .

It is very welcome to my heart just now to receive such appreciative words from my children as those I received from you on Monday, the 19th. inst., the day before my birthday. I have felt rather depressed lately, contrasting myself with some clever women, and also because of some of the mistakes I have made through yielding to the shrinking of my natural disposition and the fear of men. I know it is a kind of pride that makes me shrink from more intellectual people . . .

Then I feel some of you have suffered in your education. We ought to have done better, and yet I remember how difficult it was to pay the school bills. Well, the Lord has been very good in the way He has prospered most of you in spite of all my mistakes.

I remained home on Sunday morning and had a quiet time of communion with the Lord, and He showed me the infinite value of the blood of Christ to cover all my sin and imperfection: 'How much more shall the blood of Christ, who through the eternal Spirit offered himself without blemish unto God, cleanse your conscience from dead works to serve the living God . . .'

One can believe in the past being forgiven, yet one is sorry for misused opportunities gone for ever.

Written by Amelia Hudson Broomhall in 1898, when all her children were grown up, and four of them were already missionaries in China.

1. Always a Back-room Girl

Amelia Hudson Broomhall

It was time to lay the table for dinner. Amelia closed the exercise book in which she had been writing, stacked the lesson books and pencil box on top of it and placed all on the shelf behind the little crimson curtain hanging at the bottom of the bookcase. It was empty, as always, ready for any emergency that required the quick clearing of the table. Then she took a cloth from the chest of drawers, and opened it out over the table, humming as she did so. The best china gleamed softly in the cabinet as the sun shone into the corner where it stood, and from the kitchen floated up appetizing odours of roast lamb and mint and baked potatoes. She was pleasantly hungry, she had enjoyed her geography lesson, and in four months' time she was going to boarding school, an exciting prospect for a girl of thirteen whose mother had hitherto been her only teacher, the table her only desk.

Not that Amelia was dissatisfied with that state of affairs. Most of the other tradesmen's daughters in Barnsley received their schooling in much the same way, and had it not been that Aunt Hodson at Barton-on-Humber ran a small school for girls, Amelia would probably have completed her education at home. As it was, however, it had been arranged that she should go to Aunt Hodson as a boarder in her school, and already her mother was talking about the new clothes she would make for Amelia to take with her. Altogether, she was feeling very happy that May morning in 1849.

Then the tinkle of the shop door bell reminded her of Hudson. Was he serving or had a customer just left? She knelt quickly on the sofa to peer through the little window into the dim interior of the shop, where huge glass bottles filled with coloured liquid cast green and purple shadows across the wooden counters. Amidst the scales and the boxes and the small, carefully marked drawers of the chemist's shop she saw her brother standing with a clean white apron fastened securely around him, and one glance at his face brought a shadow over her own. The polite smile with which he had bid the departing customer 'Good day' had faded, and instead there was the discontented, almost sullen expression that had become habitual when he thought no one was looking at him.

Amelia slipped off the sofa, her forehead slightly puckered. Hudson was so unhappy. He managed to put on a cheerful face when his parents were around, but when he was alone with her he ceased to disguise his feelings. Life was irksome to him with Bible reading at table after breakfast and supper, chapel on Sunday, and the only visitors to the house being members of the family or father's preacher friends. He wanted something different sometimes, wanted to do the sort of things the young fellows at the bank did. He wished he had the money to own a horse and go hunting. He wanted a bit of gaiety in his life. He sometimes wondered if those young companions of his were right when they said there was no God. He didn't want to worry his parents, for he loved them, but however hard he tried he couldn't be their sort of Christian.

Amelia knew exactly what was the matter with him. He had no faith. He needed to be converted. That was the phraseology which she was accustomed to, and understood. When Hudson talked about the inconsistencies of professing Christians making him sceptical of what they were supposed to believe, she did not really know what he was talking about. God was God, and nothing anyone did could alter that. There were times when you felt unhappy, and that

12

God wasn't with you, but that didn't mean He wasn't there. You usually found out that it was your own fault, and as soon as you admitted you'd been bad-tempered, or deceitful, or disobedient, and asked Him to forgive you, your happiness returned. If only Hudson could see this and act on it, all his misery would go.

She had found that arguing with him about it left him completely unconvinced, so she had decided to get at him another way. She would pray for him every day. She would pray three times every day that God would convert him. She made a note of it in her little private diary. Praying twice a day was simple, because everyone in the Taylor family did that beside their beds morning and evening, on their knees. Praying secretly the third time was a little more difficult, but Amelia always managed it. There were a few minutes to go before dinner now, so she quickly opened the door leading to the stairs, sped up and dropped down by her bed.

'Oh, Lord Jesus, I pray Thee, save my brother . . .' And as she prayed the conviction came that it was going to happen, quite soon.

A short time later their mother went away on a visit to relatives, and it was during her absence that Hudson said quietly one day,

'I've got something to tell you, Amelia. It's a secret. You must promise not to say anything about it to anyone, or I shan't tell you.'

Of course Amelia promised. To be the recipient of a secret was a coveted honour, especially when it was her adored elder brother who was prepared to divulge it. Of course she would keep his secret, she would not tell a soul. Breathlessly she listened as he told her how, last Saturday afternoon when the shop was closed, he had nothing to do and so had taken a little booklet out of his father's library and gone off to read it in the storeroom at the bottom of the garden. He had known that it would have a story to begin with, and a moral at the end, and he had decided to read the story and skip the moral; but in fact he had read it all, and that very afternoon, alone in the storeroom, he had knelt down and asked the Lord Jesus Christ to be his Saviour.

Everything was different now, and he wanted Amelia to know. He was so happy. But she must keep the news to herself, a dead secret, until after mother had returned. He wanted to be the one to tell her, and to do it personally, so until then Amelia must keep quiet.

Amelia kept quiet. There was an inherent reticence about her which prevented her from even telling him about her private daily prayers for him. He discovered it for himself one day when, picking up her little diary in mistake for his own, his eye caught his own name in her writing and before he could stop himself—after all, diaries are sacrosanct—read to the end of the sentence. He had always been very fond of Amelia, but the knowledge he accidentally gained that day knit him to her on a deeper level.

There was an unusually close bond between that brother and sister which remained throughout their lives, although very soon their paths were to separate—quite how widely, neither of them could have guessed at the time. As far as they knew their separation would merely be Amelia's departure for school, but until that time came they decided they must work together to propagate their faith. It was not good enough to enjoy Bible study and prayer meetings and hymn singing, all in the company of like-minded people and with the approval of those who encouraged their fervour. They must *do* something. So on Sunday evenings the two of them set out directly after tea, armed with gospel tracts, to go from door to door in the back streets, and down dark narrow passages that led to the stuffy kitchens of poor lodging houses. If Amelia instinctively shrank from the dirt and coarseness she encountered there, she tried not to show it, though she kept very close to Hudson as he led the way.

Their parents supported them whole-heartedly in these evangelistic enterprises. By present-day standards life at home was very strict, with their father's stern insistence on punctuality,

'If you keep five people waiting for one minute, you have wasted five minutes of precious time which you can never redeem!'

on self control,

'There will be times when you will have to say "no" to yourself, and it will be difficult, so start to practise now. Why not go without a second helping of your favourite pudding?'

on scrupulous honesty,

'Pay your debts the very day they fall due. If you let them stand over for only a week, you are defrauding your creditor of interest.'

on self-reliance,

'Certainly you may have pocket money. But you must earn it by doing something. You can clean shoes, or sweep the shop, or hem dusters . . . Pocket money if you earn it—not otherwise.'

And Amelia long remembered the Sunday afternoon when she was sent to bed because she had left something she didn't like on her plate at dinner.

When it came to furthering the kingdom of God, however, no obstacles were placed in their way. Mr Taylor himself was a local preacher in the Methodist circuit and had a class of fifty or more boys whom he taught weekly. He encouraged young men to go out preaching, among them Benjamin Broomhall, apprentice to a local tailor and a friend of Hudson's. When Hudson's interest in China blossomed into the conviction that God had called him to go there as a missionary, his parents did nothing to try and dampen his enthusiasm. They encouraged him in his efforts to gain information about the country, and when he eventually obtained a copy of Luke's gospel in Chinese his father pored over it as eagerly as Hudson.

Amelia by this time was away at school. It was quite a small school, and the boarders so few they all lived with the headmistress, Amelia's aunt, sitting round the table for meals as one family, teachers and all. Conversation was subdued, laughter controlled, and all the rules of a well-bred Victorian household upheld. Amelia, in common with other young ladies of her day and age, suffered from headaches from time to time, about which her mother gave her practical advice.

'If your old companion the headache troubles you, you had better take one or two of the C.I. powders. Your aunt is very busy, by thinking for yourself and others you can relieve her.'

'Try to keep your mind calm, free from unnecessary excitement,' was another motherly adage, 'and make all your engagements the subject of prayer. Nothing which is our duty is too insignificant to bring before God.'

Those regular weekly letters from home, which arrived in neatly addressed envelopes, sealed with wax and stamped with the letter T, were eagerly looked for and read over and over again. Communications were few and precious in 1850. The penny post had been instituted only ten years and letters were treasured. All her life Amelia preserved some of those she received when at school. Her mother wrote in faultless style, telling of simple home affairs—three photos of well-known preachers had been cut out of the Wesleyan Times, framed and placed over the mantelpiece in the front room; of local happenings—there had been a fire in a nearby public house, a local tradesman was moving and had sold all his stock. Births and deaths in families she knew were recorded, and sometimes matters of grave concern were referred to, though with great reservation.

'When I look at the mistakes and misfortunes of so many around me, it makes me tremble for my own child (particularly while she is absent from me) lest in an evil hour she too should fall into the snare of the fowler,' Amelia read one day in the quiet security of the boarding school for young ladies from which she never emerged without an escort. 'I should then indeed go down in sorrow to the grave. The very thought makes me weep, and I must check the gloomy imagination.'

That Amelia's correspondence was sometimes in a lighter vein may be inferred from the concluding sentences of one of those maternal letters,

'Hudson wishes me to say he hopes you will not be long before you write to allay his anxieties on the subject mentioned in his letter last week. I expect he is full of his nonsense, and as such you must take it.'

Hudson's nonsense had sometimes upset Amelia as a little girl, when her brother teased her to the point of tears. She was better able to parry it now, and could do so in a high-spirited manner on occasion. His nonsense seems to have given him more trouble than it gave her at this stage. He became very sensitive about it, judging by the way he referred to it in one of his letters to her.

'I so often give way to temptation. I am apt to be frothy and giddy, and I sometimes yield to my teasing disposition.' Then he continued in a way which revealed a depth of spiritual longing which would have mystified a lighter-minded person than his serious little sister. 'Pray for me, Amelia, pray for me. I am seeking entire sanctification. Oh that the Lord would take away my heart of stone and give me a heart of flesh! ... My heart longs for this perfect holiness.' It was an unusually ardent and mature correspondence between the teenage boy and his schoolgirl sister. The freedom with which they could express to each other their spiritual longings bound them together. Their young souls expanded as they revealed their inner experiences and prayed fervently for each other. It is impossible to assess to what extent the quality of character and Christian maturity both revealed later was due to this enriching relationship in the formative years of their lives. The complete confidence they had in each other provided them with an inner security without which Hudson, in particular, in the bewildering and lonely experiences of his early years in China, might have floundered.

Not that things always went smoothly or without emotional disturbances. Very little is known about Amelia's

17

schooldays beyond the fact that she became very attached to a charming young music teacher, only a few years older than herself, often referred to in letters as 'Miss V.' 'Miss V.' was invited home to Barnsley for a holiday, with disastrous results for the susceptible Hudson, who fell in love with her. It was not altogether easy for Amelia to see that she now ranked second instead of first in his affections, and perhaps it involved her in a secret struggle with herself before she could accept the situation and prove an ally in his cause. An ally she certainly became. Hudson was eighteen years old by this time, and already determined to go to China as a missionary. His youth and lack of academic qualifications would have precluded him from acceptance by the five societies that already had workers in the Treaty Ports of Canton, Ningpo, Fuchow, Amoy and Shanghai. In any case, he was a Methodist, and the Wesleyan Missionary Society had no work in China. However, he was in touch with a small organization called the Chinese Evangelisation Society, which had been collecting money and sending it to Hong Kong for the support of the independent missionary work of Dr. Gutzlaff in Hong Kong. This might be the means by which he could be sent to China and supported there.

But what of 'Miss V.'? If she were prepared to marry him, who would support her? Amelia, to whom of course he had revealed his passion, considered the matter carefully, then wrote to make the practical suggestion that he should ask the Society whether they would be prepared to support a wife as well. Hudson didn't think this was a good idea. 'They would naturally conclude that I wanted to get married without means,' he explained. In any case, he did not know if Miss V. loved him. What did Amelia think? Amelia, from close observation of Miss V. and such conversation as they had together, came to the conclusion that Hudson stood a good chance. The matter was a subject of correspondence between brother and sister for some months, but was eventually dropped when it became evident that Miss V.

was interested enough in the Barnsley chemist's son to accept him as a suitor, but only if he gave up the idea of going to China. Otherwise—no.

Meanwhile, Amelia's sixteenth birthday was approaching and Hudson decided to give her a treat. He was planning to go to London to meet a German missionary who had recently returned from China, and would take Amelia with him. Most conveniently the Great Exhibition was opened about this time, and excursion trains with reduced fares were running up to the metropolis. An artist uncle living in a boarding house in Soho arranged for them to stay there with him, and there followed for Amelia what was the highlight of her young life—a week in London.

She had never been there before. Whether she actually saw Queen Victoria and her consort is not recorded, but it is certain that her kindly uncle took her around to see the sights, including the newly opened British Museum within a few minutes walk of his home. She saw the coaches of the wealthy conveying dignified gentlemen and elegantly dressed ladies, clip-clopping along the broad thoroughfares of Regent's Park and Piccadilly, the bands playing in the park, and the magnificent homes on Park Lane, although it is doubtful if she ever caught more than a glimpse of the filthy narrow back streets and yards of Dickens' London. A Victorian uncle would have shielded an innocent young niece from anything so sordid. She must be shown only the splendid sights, the most wonderful of all being the fabulous Crystal Palace, that masterpiece of cast iron and glass dominating the Great Exhibition in Hyde Park. It was Hudson who took her there, on her birthday, and after wandering among the fairy-like scenes set among ferns and flowers, he crowned it all for her by taking her to a restaurant where they were served, among other delicacies, with a pineapple.

It was not the only place to which he took her, though. She accompanied him to the office of Mr. George Pearse, the businessman who was also the secretary of the Chinese

Evangelisation Society. The outcome of that brief meeting was an invitation to them both to the north London suburb of Tottenham on the following Sunday. In that secluded area was grouped a little colony of devout Christian families, all of whom attended what was called the Brook Street Meeting. Among those well-to-do, cultured people with their large, well-appointed homes and spacious lawns, the Yorkshire schoolgirl whose family lived over a shop might have felt gauche and awkward, but Amelia acquitted herself well. As Hudson responded to the questions put to him about China and his hopes of going there, she sat demurely by, catching his eye from time to time, obviously conversant with the subject he was talking about. She made as good an impression in her way as he, and links were formed that day that were to last a lifetime.

As it happened, someone else they knew had come to live in London. Benjamin Broomhall, the young apprentice to the tailor in Barnsley, had been drawn to the metropolis with its opportunities for further education, and for hearing lectures and sermons by the most eminent men of the day. A good-looking, well-groomed, attractive young man was Benjamin Broomhall, with his broad forehead and smiling eyes, one who took life seriously but enjoyed it nevertheless. He worked hard enough at his trade during the day, but his evenings were filled with other activities. In one week his diary recorded having gone to a meeting for young men on Monday, a lecture on 'Conscience and the Bible' on Tuesday, a public meeting on Wednesday, a devotional meeting on Thursday—'which I make it a matter of conscience to attend'—a class meeting on Friday, another large meeting on Saturday, and of Sunday he wrote, 'Doctors Guthrie and Candlish from Edinburgh are announced to preach within a few minutes walk from here, and I intend to hear them.' When he was not at meetings he was in his room reading. He was only a couple of years older than Hudson and they had known each other even before Hudson came to London as a medical student at the London Hospital in Whitechapel. From that time their friendship was sealed. Its value to Hudson and to the Mission he brought into being was not to be fully realized until more than twenty years had passed.

Meanwhile Amelia's schooldays were drawing to a close when an unexpected death in the family plunged her into a new responsibility. The wife of a clergyman uncle died, leaving a little family of small children with no one to look after them. The widower's thoughts turned to his niece who was nearly seventeen and would soon be leaving school. Would Amelia come and run his home for him? She was young, but he knew her well enough to be confident that she could fit into the situation. Dodsworth, where he lived, was not far from Barnsley, so she would be near her own home and able to obtain her mother's help and advice. What did her parents feel about it?

There was no doubt in anyone's mind about where Amelia's duty lay. To Dodsworth she went, straight from school, to act as mistress in the vicarage and as mother to her small cousins. She was there when Hudson, who wrote frequently from London, sent the startling news that the Chinese Evangelisation Society was prepared to send him to China, and were suggesting that he should go as soon as he could obtain a passage on a ship going there.

Hudson actually going to China! The prospect had been before her for some years now, but that the realization of his dream was at hand, and that it meant saying goodbye to him for years—perhaps for ever—came as a shock.

In these days of radio and television when we see the ends of the earth in our homes at the press of a button, and have the world at our doorstep by means of air travel, it is difficult to realize what it must have felt like to say goodbye to someone going to China in the 1850s. The journey there must be by passenger or freight ship, round South Africa and up through the East Indies, taking several weeks at the best, possibly several months, and at worst might end in shipwreck with no other vessel near enough to come to the rescue. Letters travelled no quicker that the fastest ships could take them, and there was no other way by which private individuals could communicate with each other. So when in September 1853 Hudson Taylor boarded the little sailing ship *Dumfries* bound for Shanghai, it was almost as though he had set off for another planet.

Nearly six months elapsed before the *Dumfries* eventually berthed in Shanghai, and it was not until April or May that Amelia received her first letter from him, written the day after he arrived in China. He was a voluminous correspondent, writing fully to the Secretary of the Chinese Evangelisation Society as well as to his parents and friends, but as always it was to Amelia that the ardour of a deeply affectionate nature flowed instinctively in his hours of loneliness.

On one occasion he wrote,

You are indeed my Amelia, Amelia *Hudson,* and I feel more than a brother's love for you, he wrote on one occasion. If I could I would exercise more than a father's care for you, but I cannot. He to Whom I daily and hourly commend you, can and will . . . No words can tell the intense fervency of my love to thee, my sister. I love you more than life—whether it is right or wrong I know not. I long for your growth in grace and advancement in holiness more than for my own, not that I do not long to be more like my adorable Redeemer. I can believe from my own feelings what Paul meant when he said he could wish himself accursed for Israel's sake. And though this is such an awful thing I dare not think of it, I feel that if you might enjoy the greater I could be satisfied with the less, even of spiritual blessing . . .

He longed for her to join him, and she often wondered if that was what she ought to do. An eloquent preacher pressing the urgency of the need to carry the gospel to the uttermost parts would move her deeply, then the thought of what it would mean to her mother if she went subdued her. She had suffered so much, and was still suffering in the separation from Hudson, that to put her through it again would seem too cruel. Yet Hudson needed a companion. What ought she to do? The inner conflict lasted off and on for years, for the one overriding element needed to bring her to the point of decision seemed to be missing. The compulsive urge from God that had moved her brother to leave home and country was lacking in her case.

The lack of it puzzled her sometimes, for there was no doubt about the depth of her interest in Hudson's life and activities. His letters were read over and talked over constantly, and their contents shared with any who showed concern. It was this evident concern on the part of Benjamin Broomhall that first drew her to him—his involvement with her brother. Had it not been for that their paths might easily have diverged when young Broomhall's apprenticeship in Barnsley came to an end and he left for a job in Bradford, and later moved to London. He visited Barnsley occasionally to see his married sister who lived there, but it was his interest in Hudson that knit him to the Taylor family. As time went on, however, it was Hudson's sister who proved for him an even stronger attraction. She was in her twenties now, charmingly mature in a way, with her housewifely responsibilities in her uncle's home to claim her, rather quiet but animated enough when merry tunes were played (she enjoyed them very much, though had qualms of conscience afterwards, fearful lest she was becoming worldly) or when something stirred her to a flash of indignation. And he could not but notice the warm, shy glances with which she responded to remarks he addressed to her—in the company of others, of course. His behaviour was just what was expected of a Victorian gentleman. All the same, he was pretty sure of his ground when he wrote a decorous letter from London to Mr. Taylor, asking his permission to enter into a correspondence with his daughter, the likely outcome of which would be matrimony.

Not that young Mr. Broomhall put it quite like that, but he did not appear to have any anxiety that his letter would meet with a negative response, concluding it with the words, 'I now leave this to you and Mrs. Taylor and calmly await your reply, feeling its importance but without perturbation of mind.' Such confident composure may have struck Mr. Taylor, who was cast in a different mould, as somewhat lacking in ardour, for he waited nearly a week before replying, but when he did so his long letter, full of wise comments on the state of matrimony, ended by giving permission to 'my dear sir' to write to his daughter Amelia.

It was tantamount to an engagement and Hudson, away in China, had a sickening sense of disappointment when the news of it reached him. The possibility of Amelia's joining him had buoyed him up in many a lonely hour, and now that hope was gone.

'For the last ten years I have hoped to have you with me in China; now you have disappointed me, you know not how much. This week this thought has sometimes come over me with such force that I have felt almost heartbroken,' he wrote to her, much to her distress. Some time later, however, it occurred to him that she might yet come, with her husband who, after all, was one of his best friends. He did not fail to press the urgent needs of China when writing to Benjamin, and Benjamin was seriously considering the matter, that was evident from his letters to Amelia. How did she feel about it, he asked? For himself he felt missionary work the noblest in the world, and if he were assured that he was qualified for it, physically and spiritually, that would go far in settling things for him.

So for Amelia the uncertainty continued. China, it seemed, was forever sounding in her ears, yet when she thought of it she found herself crying, she scarcely knew why. She was not crying because of Hudson and his loneliness, she was not crying at the prospect of leaving family and friends behind if she and Benjamin went to

China. The tears came unbidden by any conscious emotion or foreboding, and she could not understand it.

'Ought we to go? Ought we not to go? Why cannot we settle it?' she wrote. 'May the Lord guide us aright. If we make up our minds to go we must prepare ourselves for a life of hardship and privation. We could bear this if we were quite sure we were in the proper place, doing what the Lord would have us. I have counted the cost,' she continued, having sombrely faced every grim possibility she could think of. With so many diseases and privations to contend with, and no doctor to call on, anything might happen. One of them would probably die young, leaving the other. 'We cannot hope both to go together, whether here or abroad, and sad and empty would that heart be that is left behind though for a little while. Still, what is life compared with eternity?'

However, the sacrifices she was prepared to make and the griefs she was prepared to endure were not required of her. 'I have committed myself to serving God as He shall ordain, either in the common duties of life or a more extended field,' she wrote, and eventually the inner conflict was solved. Benjamin gradually reached the conclusion that overseas missionary work was not his calling, and that settled it as far as she was concerned. If it was not his calling, then it was not hers either. If God was not leading him to go to China, then He was not leading her there. Meanwhile Hudson had met Maria Dyer and after a tumultuous courtship was preparing to marry her. No longer need Amelia be worried about his loneliness, and at last she could settle down. It was to 'the common duties of life' that God was calling her.

Her own engagement lasted much longer than Hudson's, and ran quietly and smoothly. The knowledge she and Benjamin gained of each other was mainly through the letters they exchanged. He told her of his activities in preaching, in committee work, and how he did not want his secular business to demand too much of his time and strength, leaving no opportunity for what he called 'direct spiritual enterprise. I am resolved to be, God helping me, a useful and an intelligent man, and nearly every book, if not every book, I have bought for some time, has been bought because I considered it to have a direct bearing on this purpose.'

She asked his advice on such matters as whether or not it was right to refuse to drink wine, even for a toast; what he thought about comic songs; how she had been trying to crucify herself by endeavouring to please and benefit others, and admitted that 'sometimes I have found it difficult, and particularly where I have not met with the gratitude which might reasonably have been expected.' She told him of the anxiety she and her parents felt over Hudson as month after month went by with no word from him, only news of much fighting in the second opium war. Benjamin was indignant over the cause of that war—it was a national disgrace. They shared as much as it is possible to clothe with words the inexpressible, their spiritual experiences, their consciousness of their Master's love, their ardent desire to please him.

As for their marriage, that could wait.

I think our love is more like a quiet little river than a dashing boisterous sea, it runs along almost imperceptibly, but the current is there for all that; only try to stop it by putting a dam across its course, and you will soon see its power; it will gather and accumulate its strength until it either bursts its bonds or runs over them. Now, I fancy we are something like this. While all goes smoothly, there is no need for a great demonstration, but only let someone try to stop us, and they will see what metal we are made of,

wrote Amelia. Meanwhile, Benjamin was working and saving to prepare a home for her, and when that time came they would be united.

She was married to him in February 1859, when she was twenty-four, and moved to Bayswater in London.

*   *   *

The smallest of all the many letters that Amelia treasured, found among her belongings after she died, was written on a piece of flimsy pink paper, tucked into a minute envelope less than three inches wide, addressed to Mrs. B. Broomhall and dated 31 March 1860. In it was revealed something none of her children knew, for they always thought that Gertrude was the eldest of them. But in that first year of married life one was conceived who never grew to infancy, and it was while she was grieving over the loss of that baby that the letter from a friend reached her.

I know that it is very dull and trying to have a recovery without any baby to interest you and fill your thoughts. It seems very sad to have had all the pain and trouble and nothing left to recompense you for it. But you have not suffered for nothing. Your infant is now added to that happy throng redeemed by the Saviour's blood, who have never lived to grieve their Lord, nor suffered the pains and trials of life. God has honoured you in making you the originator of an everlasting existence and doubtless He will not leave that child in ignorance of the source to which it owes its being, so that by it your own and its father's happiness will be forever increased.

To Amelia, with her consciousness of eternity, that little piece of flimsy pink paper contained a message that sunk deep comfort into her heart.

It was shortly after this that Hudson returned from China and his arrival, to which she had looked forward so eagerly, brought with it an unexpected reaction. The brother to whom she had meant so much before had changed. His delight at seeing her again was all she could have wished, but it soon became evident that she was no longer the main object of his ardent affection. It was on Maria and their baby girl that his eyes came to rest when they were all together, in a hundred indefinable ways the deep bond between him and his young wife were revealed. Perhaps it was because she was still emotionally disturbed that Amelia felt this so keenly. What Hudson had suffered on hearing of her engagement she now suffered on seeing him with his wife.

She got over it, of course, and never harboured any resentment against the guileless Maria, but the memory of her sense of desolation at that time deepened the sensitiveness of a naturally sympathetic nature. It was a period of her life when pain had to be endured out of sight.

Although Hudson and Maria remained in England for five years, until the formation of the China Inland Mission and the sailing to China of the *Lammermuir* party, Amelia saw comparatively little of her brother. The Hudson Taylors lived in the East End of London, the Benjamin Broomhalls in the West End. Hudson's days were filled with revision work on the Chinese Bible, with correspondence, meetings, interviews thrown in. Occasionally he would walk or travel on top of a horse-drawn bus to visit his sister, but he had neither time nor money to do it often. As for her, motherhood soon made increasing demands on her, for the birth of Gertrude in 1861 was followed by another child, then another, then another. With very little help in the house, and with four children under five to look after, she might have decided she was too busy to be responsible for the women's meeting in the local church, but 'I took it with much fear and trembling, feeling myself quite incompetent for such a task, but now after a little trial I feel encouraged to go on.' So she wrote in her diary and continued, 'I am determined by God's help no longer to live for myself, but to spend my life doing good and making happy all those who come within my reach.'

To her diary she confided her personal problems, and a major one was her inability to manage the children properly.

> I have prayed sincerely for God's help and wisdom to guide me in this matter, and I feel sure He will so long as I depend on Him. I think while they are still very young I can best accomplish my purpose by gaining their love; for this I must often sacrifice my own ease and comfort. I have begun to have prayer with them directly after tea; this will establish a habit from which I trust they will profit in years to come.

The sacrifice of her own ease and comfort was the unspectacular way in which she could best fulfil her calling to serve her Master in the common duties of life.

She determined to teach each child individually, as well as collectively, what it meant to pray. One at a time they would be brought to her room, seated comfortably, then she would say, 'I am going to talk to Jesus.' With eyes closed she would pray aloud, simply enough for the child to understand, sincerely enough for God to listen. If she was conscious of having been impatient in the child's presence she would confess it to God, asking His forgiveness and praying for help to be more patient in the future. If there were difficulties in the home, or in the father's business life, very quietly she would ask for guidance to deal with them. She told God how grateful she was for all the kindness He showed her. There was a depth of emotion in Amelia's prayers, and sometimes tears would flow—tears not so much of sorrow or of joy, just tears of tenderness. The children knew that when their mother was talking to God, she was talking to Someone she loved.

For the next fourteen years motherhood was her chief role in life. While Hudson and Maria returned to the tumults and the triumphs, the sorrows and the strains of the infancy of the Inland Mission in China, she and Benjamin lived quietly in Bayswater, where seven of their children were born. It was during this period that she had the supreme spiritual experience of her life.

She saw the Lord.

It happened when she was asleep, in a dream. She was standing in a cornfield that had just been reaped, and the winnowing process was going on. The wheat was being separated from the chaff. Then, as she looked, she saw a cloud in the sky, bright and gleaming, and she saw it was coming down, down to where she stood, and in it she saw a Figure. Beside her on one side was her husband, and on the other side Harriet the cook, and catching their hands in hers she felt herself lifted up in an ecstasy towards the Figure in the cloud, and then she saw His face . . .

She very rarely spoke of it, and could never describe that blessed face. She only knew that more than anything else she longed to see it again.

*　　*　　*

Shortly after that they moved to Godalming in Surrey, where three more children were born, bringing the number up to ten. In days when child mortality was high the Broomhalls all seemed to thrive. The family's finances had improved, for Benjamin had a good job with a firm that, among other things, supplied suits for the boys at Charterhouse. With a spacious house, large garden, pleasant countryside, and a governess for the younger children, life moved quietly and happily for Amelia.

How differently things had turned out for Hudson! Maria had died, and six of the nine children she had borne him. The cost of bringing into being the China Inland Mission had been great in human suffering, but there was no denying the fruitfulness of it. In spite of riots and dangers and privations the work of the Mission was expanding, requiring an established headquarters in England. This had now been obtained in north London, on the borders of Islington, and had been chosen largely on account of its proximity to the

Mildmay Conference Centre, which had become a centre of evangelical activity. Hundreds of people attended the conference meetings, and those who were interested in China had only to walk about fifty yards to the tall, narrow terraced house in Pyrland Road. And many people were becoming interested in China. The secretarial and financial side of the work, essential for the support of missionaries on the field and the recruiting of new members, was increasing, and the need for permanent home staff was urgent.

Thus unexpectedly the call for which Benjamin and Amelia had been prepared in their youth came to them in middle life. Amelia was forty, Benjamin forty-six. They had long since relinquished any thought of going to China, but Hudson had not given up hope that somehow they would join his work.

Now the time had come. The smooth running of the Mission in China depended on steady and reliable support at home, just the loving, inspired, faithful support his sister and her husband could give. Were they willing for it?

They had ten children under fifteen, and Benjamin would be leaving a career in which he was established with a steady income to join a mission with no visible means of support, and yet with very strict principles about not soliciting funds and not going into debt. But they had no doubt as to the rightness of the course they were taking. Three months after the birth of their last child they left the pleasant house in Surrey and moved into 2 Pyrland Road, London N.16. It adjoined the two houses that had already been acquired by the Mission, and with communicating doors linking the three together it became virtually one building, the home, not merely headquarters, of the C.I.M.

*   *   *

There was no doubt about it, Benjamin was in his element. Never had he been busier and never had he been happier. He was at Mission business from morning to midnight, either at his desk dealing with correspondence or emerging from the front door immaculately clad, his bushy beard trimmed to perfection, off to keep an appointment or speak at a meeting. Sometimes he was invited to address a company gathered for breakfast in a house where a butler relieved him of cloak and hat and ushered him in to sit among titled people. Sometimes he was off with a team of missionaries on deputation, going to small missions in the country as well as to large meetings in town halls. With his innate social ease and courtesy this son of a Staffordshire farmer could adapt himself to any company, and he was a born crusader. The social as well as the spiritual implications of political moves affected him strongly, and he waged an unceasing campaign to stop the flow of opium into China. He was well informed. The years when as a young man he had spent his evenings attending lectures or studying in order to make himself useful were paying off now. As time went on, Mr Benjamin Broomhall was often called upon for advice or to give his opinion in committee discussions.

He always left the house just in time to arrive at his destination punctually but without a minute to spare, a habit which often worried Amelia who preferred to set off half an hour earlier than was necessary for fear of being late. Not that she often accompanied him on his journeys. She had a very low opinion of her ability for public work, and shrank from the limelight. The home was her sphere, and it was here that she shone. If there was one thing more than another that the Mission needed at that time, it was the stability of a normal, happy, well-run household. For years the headquarters at Pyrland Road had been manned, it seemed, by semi-invalids—first by Emily Blatchley, the noble young woman who had brought Hudson's family of young children home from China, and had then carried the administrative burden of the work until she died. Her place was taken by Hudson himself, who had returned from China seriously incapacitated by an injury to his back. Temporary helpers there had been, and a dedicated committee, but the day-to-day running of the Mission was carried on from Pyrland Road and had it continued without healthy, permanent staff the work at the home end would inevitably have suffered, with a detrimental effect on the missionaries in China.

The coming of the Broomhalls was like the infusion of fresh blood into a weakened body. The Mission was only ten years old, and still viewed askance, if not with open contempt, by many. There were those who were not slow to criticise its faith principles, disapprove of missionaries in China wearing Chinese clothes, and openly oppose the sending of single young women into the interior. The physical infirmities of the Mission's representatives in Pyrland Road provided further cause for unfavourable comment on the part of those who were unsympathetic.

Now that was changed. The deeply spiritual but rather sombre headquarters of the Mission now throbbed with healthy happy human life, meals were served regularly, a knock on the front door answered promptly, and visitors arriving unexpectedly were soon put at their ease, for no one seemed inconvenienced. Mr. Benjamin Broomhall, it was soon observed, seemed to know how to deal with any emergency, was prompt and thorough in replying to letters and answering queries, and was always imperturbable. Better still there was now a home, a permanent home, and a mother who was always to be found in it.

In the morning she was down in the kitchen, superintending the activities of Harriet the cook, ensuring that good tasty meals were provided as economically as possible, overseeing the domestic work, the cleaning and the washing and the mending and the ironing. Missionaries home on furlough always knew where to find her in the morning.

In the afternoon, neatly clad in a fresh frock, with a little lace cap perched demurely on her wavy hair, she was ready to receive in the drawingroom any visitors who might claim her attention. In the evening she sat quietly knitting in the room where the children were to ensure that they did their

33

homework during the appointed hour. How she managed with ten of them to look after was a mystery until you learned a few of her secrets, for although the children were boisterous enough in the back garden with its swing and horizontal bars, although they ran wild in the fields beyond the house and climbed trees adventurously, they were surprisingly quiet in the house. Mrs. Broomhall had trained them well. Lessons in the nursery had been started when they were very young, one of the most important being 'a lesson in still.' It was very simple, she explained. You just ensured that the child was sitting comfortably—for how can you expect a child to sit quietly if uncomfortable?—then all that was required of him was to watch what went on around him without uttering a sound or moving. When such a lesson was well done it deserved and received a reward, of course. Not only a smile of approbation but sometimes a sweet to pop in the mouth. How much more effective was a sweet for being still than a slap for being fidgety! As they grew older being quiet when necessary was quite easy.

With a basic family of twelve, not to mention the nurse and the governess, it was obviously simple enough to invite an extra visitor or two for meals. Sometimes, when there was an influx of candidates or missionaries home on furlough there were so many people to be seated around the table that the older children had to eat their meals standing round the sideboard. Mrs Broomhall always seemed to manage, even when there were more visitors than beds. Children could be put to sleep one at the top and one at the bottom, and sometimes even three could be accommodated if they were very small, by lying them across the bed instead of one at each end. You soon felt quite at home in such a household.

As for Mr. Broomhall, he seemed to have at his fingertips all sorts of useful information which he was not only prompt to impart but willing to transform into help. If you had been in inland China for ten years, it was very bewildering to find yourself in the busy streets of London where everyone

34

seemed in a hurry, and the horses pranced along at such a pace you had to be careful that the cartwheels didn't knock you over before you had time to move out of the way. It was helpful to have someone who could find out the time of your train back home to Scotland, and tell you which station it went from. But when he did all that and then escorted you there, saw about getting your luggage into the van, tipped the porter, bought your ticket, saw you comfortably settled in your compartment, ensured that you had all you needed for the journey including smelling salts to revive you in case of train sickness—in short treated you like a queen and made you feel like one—well, it somehow put new life into you and made you forget how shabby and old-fashioned you felt wearing the clothes you'd pulled out of the trunk you'd left behind ten years ago.

One way or another, your burdens all seemed to be eased from off your shoulders when you got to 2 Pyrland Road, near Newington Green.

For the Broomhall family, wherever they eventually scattered, it was always home for them all the time Amelia lived there. And not for them only. The day came when she was told that Hudson and Jennie, his second wife, both believed God was calling her to return to China, even though it meant leaving the children behind. The emotional strain of this for Jennie in particular Amelia could only guess, but her response to the news was spontaneous.

'If God has called Jennie to go back to China, then He has called me to look after the children,' she said. So the little Taylors were brought in to share the family life of their ten Broomhall cousins. The neighbours, not surprisingly, assumed that a new school had been opened in Pyrland Road.

During the twenty years that it remained the home base of the Mission, hundreds of young men and women arrived at its doors as candidates. It was a period of rapid growth. In 1875, when the Broomhalls joined the Mission, its membership was only 38. In 1895, when they retired and the new large four-storey building at the corner of Newington Green became the headquarters, its membership had risen to 630.

Candidates' Committees were the order of the day, when the suitability of the various applicants was discussed and their fate decided. (Candidates' Committees were the order of the day in the children's room, too, as the characteristics of each aspiring missionary came up for private review there. No one else knew of the conclusions arrived at in those very secret sessions—but they usually proved to be right.) One young woman, bewildered and disappointed at having her offer of service refused on health grounds, was surprised to discover that Mrs. Broomhall apparently did not accept the decision as final. 'Go home, get plenty of rest, build up your strength and apply again,' was the advice she privately gave. Acted upon, it resulted in the young woman sailing for China to become one of the Mission's most effective workers.

The time came when one of the candidates was Gertrude, the Broomhall's own daughter, and their eldest child. Then their eldest son applied . . . then another . . . then another. They all, in turn, set off on the long, long journey to China, and Amelia knew she could not hope to see them again for years—if ever. The strain of those partings never diminished, though she had to endure so many of them. She could not face going to the docks for the final farewell, with the anguish of watching the ship draw slowly away towards the open sea. She said her goodbyes in the hall, her little body scarcely able to contain the swelling emotion of the grief she tried to hide.

Not only four of her own children went to China as members of the Mission, but two of Hudson's as well. Parting from them was scarcely less painful than from her own, she had had so much to do with them throughout their early lives. Her steady, fervent prayers for the extension of God's kingdom in China involved a willingness to be personally involved in the answers. Prayer was not to her an

36

easy way of obtaining blessings without sacrifice, or fruitfulness without pruning. If she prayed that more missionaries would be sent to China, she must be prepared for some of those she loved the dearest to be among them.

Her children observed that her first thoughts always seemed to be towards God. Setting out for a journey, welcoming a missionary home, it was always the same. 'Let us ask God's blessing on the journey . . . Let us thank the Lord for bringing you back safely . . .' And her head would be bowed in prayer.

She had prayed for her brother in his early years in China. Now she prayed for the work of the Mission he had founded. Province after province saw the establishment of centres for the preaching of the gospel, but one remained stubbornly closed: The province of Hunan. Foreigners were not allowed to cross its borders, and for years it remained the one province without a preaching centre.

Its apparent impregnability was a challenge to Amelia, and she set herself to lay siege to that far-away citadel. She prayed. Nothing seemed to happen. She prayed again and looked for encouraging news, but none came. Not to be put off she prayed on, and when still nothing seemed to happen she spoke about it to a few like-minded friends, and they agreed to pray and even fast together. The way *must* open for Christ's messengers to enter Hunan.

The way opened. It was all very unspectacular. Two women, one a Norwegian, one a Chinese, dusty and travel-stained, walked quietly in one day, the soldiers on guard not even noticing them. After that others went in too . . .

Very unspectacular. But then, so was Amelia.

Although Benjamin Broomhall retired as Mission secretary in 1895 and the three houses in Pyrland Road were no longer the headquarters, the house where the Broomhalls lived was still the family home. Even after Benjamin died, in 1911, Amelia carried on as usual, children and grandchildren instinctively returning to her, wherever they had been. Missionaries on furlough gravitated to her, too,

37

especially on Wednesday afternoons, when it was known that Mrs. Broomhall was 'at home', eager to welcome them with tea and hot scones and dainty cakes. Missionaries, being human, enjoyed that sort of thing as she very well knew, and it paved the way for more intimate chats when personal difficulties, expectations and anxieties could be shared.

'Mrs. Broomhall, I'm worried about my boy,' one missionary confided. 'He's only seventeen, starting his first job, and we're going back to China so soon now. Where will he live then? Please pray that he may get lodgings in a Christian family.'

Mrs. Broomhall, aged just on eighty by now, did more than pray. She talked the matter over with Annie, her youngest daughter who lived at home and ran it for her.

'All our bedrooms are occupied,' she said. Three children and two grandchildren were living in the home at the time. 'But I'm thinking about that little spare room half-way down the stairs. Couldn't we make it into a bedroom for him?' So young Douglas Brock moved in as a member of the family, and his parents returned to China with their hearts at rest.

*   *   *

'There's something I want to ask you to pray about, Mrs. Broomhall,' said a young candidate as he pushed her in her bath chair round the Green. She was very frail by this time, and could not walk out unaided. The Candidates' Secretary liked her to meet the prospective missionaries, in order to obtain her opinion of them. She was a kindly but shrewd judge of character. The young man pushing her chair that afternoon had a personal problem. He was very interested in one of the girl candidates, but never had the opportunity to speak to her. Mission rules were very strict. Men and women candidates lived fifteen minutes' walk away from each other, and were kept firmly apart. The young man respected the rules, but how was he to find out if the girl he was thinking of would make him a good wife if he never even spoke to her? How could he get to know her?

Mrs. Broomhall agreed to pray. She also sent a message to the Candidates' Secretary asking if a certain young lady could be spared to come and take her for an airing on a certain afternoon. The request was readily granted. The arrival in the Green of a certain young man as she was being dutifully pushed around could not have been more timely. 'It's so pleasant here in this sunny spot, I really think I'd like to stay here for a while,' she said after greeting him. 'Why don't the two of you go off for a walk, and come back in half an hour to push me home?'

*   *   *

Amelia was sitting in the drawingroom one evening during the early months of the Great War, when her granddaughter arrived home from the War Office, where she was patriotically 'doing her bit'.

'Grandma, it doesn't pay to be a Christian,' the girl said indignantly. The head of department was always finding fault with her because she was a Christian, she went on to explain. If she was half a minute late for work he was down on her, but another girl could be away for an hour or more, picking up bargains at the sales, and he only laughed when she returned in the middle of the afternoon, and showed her purchases around. 'It's not fair. He wouldn't be down on me if I weren't a Christian.'

Amelia called her over to sit beside her, picked up her Bible and opened it at the seventy-third psalm. 'Many people have felt like you do, my dear,' she said gently and pointed to the words.

'Behold, these are the ungodly, who prosper; they increase in riches. Verily I have cleaned my heart in vain and washed my heart in innocency . . . When I thought to know this, it was too painful for me; until I went into the sanctuary of God; then understood I their end . . . They are brought unto desolation in a moment.'

The girl read the words silently, looked up at her grandmother, gave a little nod and went quietly out of the room. Sixty years later she remembered it as clearly as if it had been yesterday. 'It was too painful for me until I went into the sanctuary of God. Then I understood . . .'

*   *   *

It was Easter Sunday morning, 1918. Very quietly a small group of the Broomhall family gathered around the breakfast table. They had nothing much to say. They were thinking of the little body lying so still now in the bedroom above, and they did not feel like talking. When the time came for the devotions which were always held after breakfast, Annie brought her mother's Bible and lay it before the brother who was sitting at the head of the table, and opened it at the fly-leaf. There, in the handwriting he knew so well, he saw the words that she must have written long ago as she looked ahead to this moment.

> I am leaving, I am leaving
>   For the country of my King:
> Let not words of grief be spoken
> Let not loving hearts be broken,
>   Rather let the joy-bells ring:
> For earth's wintry life is changing
>   Into everlasting Spring.

*   *   *

She never went to China, performed no acts of outstanding courage, had no spectacular achievements to her credit, swayed no audiences with her eloquence. Hers was an unusually sheltered life, from beginning to end surrounded by deep family love. Even at her death it was the same. Her body was carried to the grave by three of her own sons and one of Hudson's, a grandson and a son-in-law. On the face of it she has no claim to a place in the annals of a mission that has worked and suffered in the Far East for over one hundred years, and she certainly would not have claimed it for herself.

But the sum total of a mission's quality is not contained in its outward activity, any more than the value of a tree lies only in its fruit. Without the root under the ground, there would be no tree. Without the Amelias, there would be no Mission.

I feel, darling, that we *must* lean fully and constantly on Jesus if we are to get on at all, and I have been seeking to do it, and in believing prayer to bring our many needs to Him. I have written down the names of our foreign and native helpers, that I may be able to plead for them all daily. If we would have power for what Jesus calls us to do, we must not expend it in bearing burdens that He would have us cast on Him, must we? And there is abundant supply, with Him, for all the work, for all we need, isn't there? It's unbelief that saps our strength and makes everything look dark: and yet He reigns, and we are one with Him, and He is making everything happen for the very best; and so we ought always to rejoice in Him, and rest, though it is not always easy. We must triumph with God, and then we shall succeed with men, and be made blessings to them.

You know these things, and can put them much better than I can, but still it does us good to remind one another, doesn't it?

Written by Jennie Taylor to her husband during one of their many long separations.

2. Successor To Maria

Jennie Hudson Taylor

Miss Jane Faulding, known to her family and friends as Jennie, stepped lightly from the hansom cab that had brought her to 30 Coburn Street, Bow, that warm Saturday in June 1865, and hurried up the narrow strip of garden to the front door, her face aglow. She loved coming here. The Saturday afternoon prayer meeting held for the little mission in Ningpo, China, was the highlight of her week, with the friendly, eager greetings of those who gathered, the sense of anticipation as they settled into their seats, and the excitement of listening to the latest news. Mr. and Mrs. Taylor, who could embellish the reports by missionaries with intimate, colourful descriptions and explanations, made it all come alive. And the prayers and the singing and the burning challenge! The presence of the living Christ was as real as if they had been with Him back in Galilee two thousand years ago, and were hearing Him say, 'Go ye into all the world and preach the Gospel to every creature.'

Jennie had been conscious of the personal application of that command before, but it was to crystallize now. That particular Saturday prayer meeting proved to be historic, and although she did not know it, set the course for her life.

Mr. Hudson Taylor led it. He had just returned from Brighton, where he had been for a few days' rest, and looked very much better than before he went away. The long hours of revision he had put in on the Bible in the Ningpo dialect had quite drained him, but he seemed completely renewed now, and as the meeting proceeded he told them that there

43

was something he was longing to impart. God had been speaking to him again about the millions upon millions in China who were still waiting for the news of eternal salvation. As he had already told the group gathered in that narrow room, he had been studying available statistics about the population of China, and they had shared with him the burden of the knowledge that a million souls there died without Christ every month. They had been praying with him about it, looking beyond the Treaty Ports where a few little groups of missionaries were at work, to the vast hinterland of eleven provinces stretching away to Tibet and Mongolia. The country was open politically, for the treaty signed in 1860 allowed foreigners to travel and even live there now. But with no workers to go and no money to support them it had seemed impossible that anything could be done to break into the spiritual darkness of the great Chinese Empire.

It had seemed impossible—but he had been reminded that the things which are impossible with man are possible with God. To hold back now, when the door was open, was unbelief. He was therefore praying that God would send him twenty-four men and women, willing and skilful in service for God, to form the spearhead of a mission into those eleven unoccupied provinces of China, and also into Chinese Tartary and Tibet. He believed God would answer his prayer, so he had taken the practical step of opening a bank account in the name of the China Inland Mission, since the Lord, he firmly believed, would provide the money for the workers he was going to send. All reasonable preparations must be made, so that as soon as they were ready they could go to China without delay.

That was the gist of what Mr. Taylor had to say, but it in no way conveys the solemn fervour with which it was delivered, or the effect it had on those who listened.

Jennie, for one, was deeply moved. This was thrilling! A new Mission had been launched. Whatever purpose she may originally have had for the golden sovereign reposing in her purse had to go to the wind. There was only one way in which it could be used now, and she promptly gave it to Mr. Taylor as a contribution to the China Inland Mission. She evidently did not keep the news of this new society to herself, for she was back again three days later with some more money. It had been given to her to pass on, and Mr. Taylor entered it as a contribution of three shillings and sixpence from the Regent's Park Chapel. What did it matter to Jennie if it was a comparatively small amount, and she could have waited until Saturday to bring it? It had been given by people whose hearts the Lord had touched and Jennie was eager to pour it all into the coffers as quickly as possible.

Those were days of intense spiritual emotion and there was a stirring in churches and chapels throughout the land. Against the sombre backdrop of social inequalities in Victorian England, with its wealth and its poverty, its snobbishness and its servility, courageous figures were emerging to proclaim by act as well as by word what discipleship to Jesus Christ involved. They were opening medical missions and soup kitchens in the slums, disclosing the vices of the rich and the despair of the poor, urging reforms, all along with the proclamation of the Gospel. William Booth was pioneering the work which later became the Salvation Army, the Earl of Shaftesbury was fighting in Parliament on behalf of the destitute and defenceless, Charles Hatton Spurgeon was preaching his memorable sermons in the Tabernacle. All this Jennie had heard about, and a great deal more besides, but nothing moved her so much as the knowledge of those millions upon millions in China who had no opportunity to hear, not even once in a lifetime, that God's Son had died for them. She went along again and again from her comfortable home in Euston to the narrow little house in Bow. The months passed and Hudson Taylor interviewed candidate after candidate who came believing that God had called them to go with him to China, and one of those who came was Miss Jane Faulding.

The fact that most of the young men and women who were preparing to sail with Hudson Taylor's party came from a different class of society from the circle in which she moved did not affect her. What is perhaps even more surprising is that her parents were willing to let her go with what must have appeared a very heterogeneous company. In the class-bound system of the nineteenth century it was an almost unheard-of thing for artisans to mix on equal terms with those from the professions, or the daughters of well-to-do businessmen with the wives of village blacksmiths.

There were plenty of well-meaning people who questioned the wisdom of it, observing that it was going too far, that it was not good for working-class people to be taken out of their stations. What was even worse, however, was for Britons of any class whatever to go to China and actually live there like Chinese, even wearing Chinese clothes. 'Going native!' they said scornfully. 'It's a disgrace to the British Empire.' As for sending young Englishwomen right into China without any protection, there ought to be a law passed to stop it, and the man behind the whole scheme, this Hudson Taylor, ought to be forcibly restrained.

It took courage and conviction to stand against the pressure of widespread public opinion, over and above the natural pain of separation, but both Jennie and her parents were ready for it. She was one of the party of twenty-two, including the Hudson Taylor family, who sailed for China on the *Lammermuir* on 26 May 1866, eleven months after the official launching of the China Inland Mission.

*   *   *

There is an epic quality about the four-months' journey in the three-masted sailing ship that captures the imagination, even after the passing of a century. The entire passenger accommodation had been taken by Hudson Taylor in a dramatic way, shortly before the sailing date. Early one morning, while away from home, he received a letter from shipping agents telling him about it, but he knew he had insufficient money in hand to make the necessary down-payment. To his amazement his host, directly after breakfast and knowing nothing whatever about the matter, handed him a cheque for £500, saying God had been speaking to him in the night, telling him to give it.

Mr. Taylor lost no time in unnecessary reflection. This was the answer to his prayers. He went straight to the docks, looked over the ship, saw it was suitable, and handed over the cheque. The rest of the money needed came in, and his party being complete they all set sail for China and the unknown on a wave of fervent spiritual joy. They sang and they prayed and they studied Chinese, they talked and they laughed and with shining faces spoke about Christ, until the hard-bitten crew who had taken a very gloomy view of the prospect of travelling with a shipload of missionaries, were won over. These happy people, so young and friendly, leaving home and country for who knew what sort of life in the middle of China—what made them do it? By the time the voyage was half over most of the officers and crew were joining in the meetings publicly, and seeking out one or another of the missionaries privately, to find out how they, too, could become Christians. There was something apostolic about it.

Not that things went entirely without a hitch. True to human experience, the pioneers of the China Inland Mission, like the disciples of old, every now and then fell out among themselves. The blacksmith petulantly asserted that he and his wife had been insulted by this one and that one. The carpenter and the mason refused to partake of the Lord's supper with the ship's mate because he had a bad temper. The usually sunny-tempered Jennie and her bosom friend, the deep-thinking melancholic Emily Blatchley, were at one time on speaking terms of a very frigid nature.

Mr. Taylor, quietly observant, had a way of dealing with these upsets. He spoke in private, very gently, to individuals, and suggested to all that it would be a good thing to have a special meeting for confessions of failure, and for deepened unity. Harmony was restored.

So the ship sailed on. Then, as it entered the China seas, the weather changed. The wind increased, the glass fell steadily, the rain poured down and the waves raged. They were on the edge of a typhoon; as the little vessel battled its way on things got worse and worse until, as with the shipwreck so vividly described in the books of Acts, the mariners gave up hope of being saved. It was all hands at the pumps, missionaries as well as sailors, women as well as men, while the waves pounded over the decks.

Our main sail was torn to ribbons, the jib boom and fore, main and mizzen masts were carried away, and it seemed impossible we should weather it [wrote Jennie later]. I am glad to say we were all kept calm, ready for life or death. We were making water fast. The broken masts were hanging over our heads as if by a thread, swinging about fearfully and threatening every moment to fall—which if they had done, the deck or side of the vessel must have been staved in, and we should have gone down in a few minutes. I did feel so thankful that you could not know, for I had the strongest conviction that our lives would not be lost.

It lasted for a fortnight. The ship was driven off course, and when eventually the storm subsided it took five days for it to drift rather than sail near enough to Shanghai to be sighted and towed into harbour.

Storms of another kind awaited the party in Shanghai. This time the battering they received was not from the elements, but from their fellow-Europeans, who viewed with derision and indignation the arrival of this swarm of young English people, apparently devoid of any bank balances, who were preparing to dress like Chinese and in their condemnation, quoting freely the newspaper comment that this Mr. Taylor who had brought them out must be either a madman or a knave. Even most of the missionaries in Shanghai, though more guarded in what they said, disapproved of the scheme.

The prompt and generous action of an American Presbyterian, Mr. Gamble, in offering accommodation to the whole party, solved what might have proved a very embarrassing situation, for missionaries arriving in Shanghai were normally given hospitality by others of their own community. The party of eighteen adults and four children who had turned up unannounced on a boat that was little more than a wreck would have posed a problem in the most favourable circumstances. As it was, everyone was spared. Mr. Gamble, with unforgettable kindness, had them all conveyed in sedan chairs from the crowded wharf-side to the seclusion of his compound, where they were free to wash their clothes, sort out their belongings, and catch their breath before proceeding on the next stage of their journey.

For Jennie it seemed like a happy dream to be surrounded by men with *queues* and women with small bound feet. She was really in China at last, and ready to plunge straight in. Whatever misgivings some of the others may have had about the new manner of life on which they were embarking, she seems to have had none. When the men of the party donned long Chinese gowns and had their heads shaved up to the crown, from where a plait—the *queue*— was encouraged to dangle, she and Emily privately agreed that it was an improvement. The carpenters and the blacksmiths and the mason looked like gentlemen now, dressed as Chinese teachers. The only one whose appearance was not improved by the change was Mr. Taylor, who always had looked like a gentleman, anyhow. From which it may be inferred that the two young ladies were not without their preferences and prejudices. When one of the blacksmiths, irked at the thought of being like a mere 'native', reverted to western type clothes against the expressed policy of the Mission, Jennie and Emily were firmly on the side of Mr.

and Mrs. Taylor, and so throughout a series of unhappy episodes which culminated in five of the *Lammermuir* party leaving the Mission altogether.

This did not happen until they had all been in China for a couple of years, however, and although it was a grief to the Taylors in their position of leadership, it did not affect Jennie to any great extent. By this time she was one of the best-known figures in Hangchow, the beautiful old city at the head of the bay situated between Shanghai and Ningpo. It was here that Hudson Taylor had first settled with the *Lammermuir* party, and established his headquarters.

Right from the start Jennie had been a success with the Chinese. She learned their language rapidly, had no inhibitions about trying it out, wore their clothes, and ate with chopsticks with an almost childlike zest that won their hearts. She went in to chat with the women living in the same compound, took a lively interest in them and their children, and obviously enjoyed being with them. Then she told them, in the most earnest yet artless way, the good news she had for them—and they listened. Word of this young female foreigner got to the the ears of the wives of mandarins, and she received courteous invitations to visit them in their homes. Off she went. Then she was invited to a nunnery. She went there, too. And a woman here, a woman there, started to walk the Way of Life.

She wrote home,

'My heart does so well up for joy that I am here. And here among the people to a great extent as one of themselves. I should think that when I go out I often speak to more than two hundred people ... Yet I am never treated in any way rudely, but with all kindness. *Fuh Ku-niang* often wishes she could make herself into two or three, or else accomplish two or three times as much as she can in one day.'

(Jennie's Chinese name was *Fuh*, meaning happiness; *Ku-niang* was the title given to unmarried women.)

Hudson Taylor and Maria looked on with increasing wonder. Whatever might be the problems they were encountering with some of the members of their team, there were none with this one. On the contrary, she was vindicating their much-criticized action in taking single women to the interior of China. It is doubtful if it even occurred to Jennie that she was a pioneer, that no woman missionary had ever before walked around a Chinese city in the way she was, dressed as a Chinese, strolling in and out of courtyards to chat with the women there with unself-conscious ease. There were two other missions in Hangchow at the time, but all the missionaries wore western clothes, and their wives rarely left their spacious compounds except to visit each other. The men missionaries had been able to go freely to the tea-houses and talk with the men there by the hour, but the women behind the great double-leaved doors had had to be passed by. It had been one of Hudson Taylor's declared reasons for including women in his team that only they could reach the secluded members of their own sex. The decision was being justified. As he watched some of the young women at work now, especially Jennie Faulding, he knew they had something to contribute that had been lacking before. And Maria wrote, 'Had we the right people and suitable accommodation, I feel pretty sure I could find work for ten Miss Fauldings and ten Miss Bowyers. The Lord ever keep them as simple and true-hearted as they are!'

When the time came for Mission headquarters to be moved elsewhere, and for the young missionaries to be settled in other cities, Jennie Faulding had so mastered the local dialect and so endeared herself to the people of Hangchow, that it was decided to leave her there, along with Mr. and Mrs. John McCarthy. For the whole of her first term of service in China she scarcely moved from the city. It was from Hangchow that she and John McCarthy wrote the letters that led Hudson Taylor into a deepened spiritual experience of which he often spoke and wrote later, and which he exemplified in his personal life. For months he had been battling with a sense of inward failure, burdened with anxieties, weak in faith. Now came these two letters from Hangchow, each telling of a similar sense of defeat that had been transformed into victory and peace by simply believing the Lord Jesus was keeping His promise never to leave nor forsake them. The consciousness of His presence was their salvation. 'Not by striving after faith, but by resting on the Faithful One' was how John McCarthy put it, while Jennie's way of expressing it was 'looking unto Jesus'. Both meant the same thing, and it was evident they were both experiencing the same inner happiness and relief from strain. A significant turning point in Hudson Taylor's spiritual life stemmed from the day he received those two Hangchow letters.

By this time Jennie had been in China for three years. Not only had she been visiting women in their homes, but a school for little boys had been started, and this led her into the realm of administrative responsibility. 'This week the school has passed into my hands more entirely than before,' she wrote. 'It will no longer be carried on at mission expense. I have taken responsibility for its support, believing that funds will be supplied as needed.' There were twenty-one scholars, and twelve of them were boarders. 'It will save Mr. Taylor trouble, and I feel convinced it is the right thing.'

A couple of years later she started a boarding school for girls, again shouldering the financial responsibility. It was a considerable relief to have it so, especially when mission funds were low. Young Miss Faulding, not yet twenty-seven, was certainly saving Mr. Taylor trouble.

So was Emily Blatchley, though in another way. She had developed along different lines, and had become a permanent member of the Taylor household, acting as Hudson's secretary, and as guardian to the children when he and

Maria were away visiting other mission centres. It was this care for the children that eventually changed the course of her life. The eldest of them was eight years old, and it was obvious that they could not remain indefinitely in the interior of China without proper schooling, and with hazards to their health. They must return to England; the question was, who should take them?

On the face of it Maria was the one to do so, but if she went, what about Hudson? She was his closest confidante in the work and to leave him for an indefinite period would create difficulties which became more evident the more they discussed the matter. In the end Emily Blatchley solved the problem by offering to take the children herself. With a fine courage she conducted the two little boys and tiny girl halfway round the world and settled with them in England. She kept in constant touch with the Taylors, writing regularly, for she not only looked after the children, but carried most of the day-to-day work at the home end of the Mission into the bargain.

Less than a year later the news reached her that Maria had died, and Hudson was left a widower.

The news reached Jennie Faulding too, and it came as a shock to them both. As new workers they had been very close to the Taylors and had been rather like younger sisters in their home. They both knew the deep bond of love that had united husband and wife, and their natural sympathy was drawn out towards the man they regarded as an elder brother.

Undoubtedly Emily knew him the better, having lived in his home for so long. The correspondence between them continued unabated, with his children in her care as a permanent link between them. Jennie, fully and happily engaged in her own work, had less cause to write to him, but from time to time she saw him when he came to Hangchow in the course of the visits he continued to make to the Mission's various centres.

And for all three of them there came the growing

awareness of the place at his side that Maria had filled, and which was now vacant.

Eventually it was Jennie who took the place. Hudson was finding it increasingly difficult to work alone, and the more difficult he found it the more his thoughts turned to '*the only one* possessed of the heart for the Lord's service and of that peculiar preparation for sharing my peculiar duties . . .' as he expressed it. He got to the point where he was sure of his own feelings, though he tried to suppress them, but he did not know hers. Her work in Hangchow so fully satisfied her–would she want to give it up for good? Was it even right to ask it of her? He did not know.

It had already been arranged that, in response to her mother's request, Jennie should return to England for a time, together with Mr. and Mrs. Meadows. They were booked to travel on a certain ship and Hudson, who also had to return, largely on account of his children, was in a quandary. Uncertain as he was of her feelings he both longed to travel with Jennie, and yet dreaded it. At first it seemed that he would be unable to do so anyway, for the boat was due to sail before he could reach Shanghai. If it left on schedule, there would be nothing he could do about it.

The boat was delayed. He arrived at the port to find it was still there, so he booked a passage and sailed with the party.

Whatever may have been Jennie's feelings when the long sea voyage commenced, all Hudson's uneasy doubts had been dispelled by the time the ship was steaming up the Red Sea. Long quiet days on board, leisurely strolls along the deck, silent watchings together as the moon soared slowly into the heavens, prayer that seemed to flow as effortlessly as the waves that lapped against the side of the ship, all had had their effect.

'It is no small joy to me to find my love and my feelings so fully reciprocated,' he wrote to her parents, confident that their permission would be granted for him to marry their daughter.

On 26 September 1871 Mr. Hudson Taylor, Mr. and Mrs.

Meadows and children, and Miss Jane F. Faulding arrived in England, so the Mission records state briefly. Two months later it was announced that Mr. Taylor and Miss Faulding were married.

The bare facts are easily related. The intricacies of human relations are not. Most of Hudson Taylor's friends were glad that his loneliness was ended, and Jennie had already won their regard as a member of the *Lammermuir* party who had proved herself an exceptionally dedicated missionary.

For Emily Blatchley, however, painful readjustments had to be made. Her position in the Taylor household must be relinquished, and the children become accustomed to a new mother. What the marriage of her friend to the father of those children meant to her she concealed as much as possible, but there is little doubt that the grief went very deep. In some ways it was probably a relief when, after a year at home, Hudson Taylor and Jennie returned to China. Emily had agreed to resume her former role, taking charge of the mission home and the children, and she took up the reins again with quiet dedication. But not for very long. She already had tuberculosis of the lungs, and her condition worsened rapidly. Hudson and Jennie never saw her again. Three years after their marriage, she died.

Dr Gratton Guinness wrote in a tribute to her,

The most glorious triumphs of Christ are spiritual. The noblest work is that wrought in the secret of the soul. Not the conquest of kingdoms, but self-conquest; not the renunciation of anything external merely, but self-renunciation; not the consecration of substance, but self-consecration in the service of God and man—these are the hardest deeds to accomplish and the most divine attainments. They shine with the peculiar light of Calvary.

*   *   *

The growth of the China Inland Mission was marked from time to time by dramatic appeals for more workers, and one of these appeared in the north when Jennie's first child was born. She was home again in England by this time, and so was Hudson, with an injured back which kept him on his bed for nearly five months. It is worth noting that out of their general disability for active work a forward movement was launched which resulted in the sending out of what was known as The Eighteen—eighteen more young people to fan out in inland China with the news of God's salvation.

The forward movement of that period, it was freely admitted, had been made practically possible by a gift of four thousand pounds donated for that very purpose. No mention was made of the source from which the money came. Only those most intimately concerned knew that it was a legacy which Jennie had received on the death of a relative and she had quite simply handed it all over to be used by the Mission, and after consulting with Hudson decided it should go for forward evangelism.

There were plenty of reasons why she might have retained the money. With a growing family of her own (she had another child in the following year) as well as three step-children, no one would have blamed her if she had done so. One friend at least questioned the wisdom of taking such a course, and to him Hudson Taylor wrote fully, explaining their position.

As to the property my dear wife has given to the Lord for His service, I most cordially agreed with her in the step, and do so now. I believe that in so doing she has made hers for ever that which was her Master's, and only entrusted to her so to use . . . We do not propose to put either principal or interest into the general fund, but to use it, equally avoiding stint or lavishness, as the Lord may direct, for special purposes not met by the general fund. We are neither of us inexperienced, unacquainted with the value of money, or unaccustomed either to its want or possession. There are few more cool and calculating, perhaps, than we are; but in all our calculations we calculate on God's faithfulness, or seek to do so. Hitherto we have not been put to shame, nor have I any anxiety or fear lest we should be in the future.

For the next two or three years Jennie remained in England, although for a good deal of that time Hudson was in China. He had been away from home for some sixteen months when he returned just before Christmas in 1877. His two youngest children did not even remember him. It was the longest period of separation Jennie had had from him since their marriage, and with so much for him to do at the home end she looked forward to a year and more of normal home life before he set off again for China.

What was her consternation, therefore, when less than a couple of months after his return, he broached the subject of their separating again. He had had a stiff struggle with himself before doing so, for what he was suggesting was not that he should return to China in the near future: too many matters had to be settled regarding administration and candidates for that. The need in China just now was not for him. The need in China was for her.

Jennie could scarcely believe it. Hudson was asking her if she would leave him and the children and go back to China alone.

The famine there was the reason. News of it was worrying her as well as him. Away up in the north, a thousand and more miles inland, literally millions of people were starving. The number given in official statistics was six million. Foreign relief agencies were sending help and the Chinese government was doing something about it, but the need far exceeded the supply, and Hudson Taylor, with his intimate knowledge of conditions in China, was making known the facts. Not only were tens of thousands of people dying of starvation, but thousands more were being sold into slavery of the worst kind, for a morsel of bread. As always in similar circumstances, there was brisk trade in girls and young women, as merchants in human vice and misery came to obtain helpless little chattels for the brothels of the southern ports.

The need was not only for food, but for orphanages into which children could be brought for protection. Even deeper than that was the spiritual despair of those who were without Christ and without hope. In times of upheaval and famine it was usually the women who suffered the most, and to women in China only women could speak freely.

The forward movement into hitherto unreached regions was being led by men—but did the special circumstances of the famine stricken areas call more for the activity of women? And if so, who was to lead a team of young women missionaries up there and see them established in orphanage and relief work? There were those who were ready to go, but they were not only young, they were inexperienced. What was needed was a woman with spiritual maturity and the ability to take charge. She must be a woman they knew and trusted, one who could speak Chinese and who knew the people. She must be one who had initiative and could shoulder responsibility—as she, Jennie, had done when, still in her early twenties, she had taken charge of the schools in Hangchow, looking to God, not to the Mission, for their support. To go up into the famine-stricken north and establish new young missionaries there required a woman leader of courage and faith and experience. The only one Hudson Taylor knew to be in every way suitable, who could be freed from present duties, was his own wife.

Jennie faced what was probably the most painful conflict of her life when Hudson put the matter to her. If she agreed to go it would mean being separated from her children for an indefinite period, and by a two-month journey. On top of that would be the responsibility of the young workers who went with her, their health and safety, as well as decisions about where to settle and how to start work in an area to which no western woman had ever gone before. It seemed too much to ask, especially as Hudson himself was ill, weakened by his travels and trials, and she felt she could not leave him.

But those women and girls in the north of China—without hope in this world or the next . . . Her promise to her Master to follow wherever He should lead her, whatever the cost . . .

It did not take Jennie long to come to the point of being willing, though the depths of anguish to which she plunged to get there were new and strange to her. Having got there, she could view things less emotionally. She knew the way ahead would be strewn with difficulties and that faith as well as endurance would be tested, and she wanted to be quite sure that it was God himself who was commanding her to go. With that assurance she could face anything, but without it she knew she would falter. Even the complete solving of the problem of the children when Amelia Broomhall said immediately, 'If Jennie is called to go to China, then I am called to look after her children,' was not quite sufficient. Self-sacrifice might be mere heroics, a spartan-like response to a grim challenge, and not obedience to the will of God.

It was not her custom to ask for signs to confirm what she was convinced was the right thing to do, but in this case she felt she needed them. Being a practical person, and knowing they were quite low in funds, she decided the confirming signs should be for money to be given in such a distinctive way that she would know God had given it in answer to her prayers.

'Lord,' she said. 'I'll need an outfit. If it is Thy will for me to go to China, please give me some money personally, for my personal outfit.' Then she added something more. It would be a great relief to have plenty of money in hand at a time like this, not only for herself, but for those left behind. Dared she ask for quite a large, specific sum to come to

them for their own use? Dared she ask for fifty pounds?
Yes, she dared.

'Lord, wilt Thou send us fifty pounds as a further proof
that Thou art sending me? Fifty pounds just now would be
worth more than a fortune to me at another time. It would
be a guarantee that all other needs will be met. It would take
away any doubt that I am doing Thy will by going to China.
Exactly fifty pounds, Lord—sent to us, not to the Mission.'

The next day she received the answer to her first request.
A friend came to see her, and on departing asked her to
accept a little gift towards expenses connected with the
journey. The sum given was ten pounds, exactly the amount
the Mission considered necessary for an outfit. Jennie had
not told anyone, not even Hudson, about her prayer, and
kept this prompt answer to herself, almost breathless to see
if the second and larger request would be granted.

Within a week it came. A letter from Hudson's own
parents, addressed to them both, contained a cheque for
fifty pounds, and as he was cogitating on how it should be
used she almost snatched it from him. 'That's mine!' she
cried triumphantly. 'I claim it!' And then she told him why.
This was not intended for anyone else. God had sent it to
them, not to the Mission. It was His seal to her personally
that He and no one else was sending her to China.

Something else happened for which she had not even
asked. On the day before she boarded the steamer that was
to take her and a party of new workers to Shanghai she
received another letter. In it was another cheque, a gift
towards the orphanage she was hoping to open.

'Please enter it anonymously', wrote the donor, who
admitted that his business could ill afford the money that
was being taken out of it. Then he added, 'If you for Christ's
sake can separate, I cannot give less than this.'

The cheque was for one thousand pounds.

So she said goodbye to her husband, her children and her
home, and went to China. With one of the men missionaries
as an escort she went with two young women missionaries

on the long journey of over a fortnight from Shanghai to the famine stricken province of Shansi. There she remained until an orphanage was opened and the new workers established. She had become a pioneer in her own right by the time, a year later, she and Hudson were reunited in Shanghai.

It was three years before she saw her children again, although however deep her natural longing to be with them, she knew she had no cause to be anxious about them. Step-brothers, step-sisters and cousins were all living together as one big family in the Broomhalls' home. When eventually she returned to England, however, she remained with them for nine years until, in 1890, the frequent long separations from Hudson ended as she rejoined him in China.

The development and expansion of the Mission during the next decade, culminating in the debacle brought about by the Boxer rebellion, is her story as well as his. They retired to Switzerland in 1901 and in 1904 Jennie died. For over thirty years she had been married to the man who founded the Mission in which she herself was one of the most notable women pioneers. From time to time she had inherited quite large sums of money, all of which she appears to have taken the utmost pleasure in giving away, mainly to missionary societies.

She was a singularly uncomplicated, merry person. Her whole attitude towards her life was unconsciously summed up in something she wrote in a letter home during her first year in China,

'Please don't talk about my "hardships". It is a great privilege to be here. And you know, it is not even a trial to me to rough it. I only told you about our contrivances to amuse you and give you an idea of how we are getting on. We don't seek a smooth path; it is a greater joy to feel that we are pilgrims and strangers . . .'

I was wondering whether you were not lonely this morning. When I first came to China I was very lonely, and once told my mother something about it. I want to tell you what Mother wrote back to me. She said 'Live to love, and you will never be lonely. Live in the lives of others, those around you. How they need love! You will never be lonely if you live to love and love to live.' And I have found it true.

> *Written by Margaret King in the last year of her life, in a letter to a young American missionary who had just arrived in China.*

3. Not the Marrying Sort

Margaret King

In the year that Jennie Taylor left her home, husband and children to go to the famine-stricken area in north China, a young American named Henry W. Frost crossed the Atlantic to see Hudson Taylor. He had become deeply concerned about the evangelization of China, and came with the suggestion that a branch of the China Inland Mission should be formed in North America. He approved the principles and methods of the society, and would do all within his power to encourage suitable young people from his country to go out under its auspices.

Taylor did not at first think it a good idea, although later he changed his mind. Better for the Americans to form their own organization, he said. However, he was eventually persuaded to make his journey back to China via North America in order to speak about his experiences at a large convention near Niagara. D. L. Moody was among those present, and was so impressed by the practical outworking of faith in Taylor's story that he urged him to come up to Canada and repeat his talk there.

That is how he came to Montreal and how Margaret King's life was changed.

Margaret was the eldest daughter in a big family of boys and girls, but she did not see much of them, except during holidays. Her grandmother brought her up, and although strict she gave her, on the whole a very good time. Intelligent, bright-eyed Grandmother Yuile had plenty of money and enjoyed travel, especially to Europe, so off she

63

went; when Margaret grew into her teens, she took her along too. They were sometimes away for months on end, and when they returned Margaret's wardrobe was enriched by smart gowns from Paris. A very elegant young lady she looked in her long seal coat, with diamond rings sparkling on her fingers, and her dark eyes aglow.

She thought she was reasonably happy until she met Hudson Taylor, and then she realized she was not. Deep within her was a longing for something, she knew not what, and this slight, quiet little Englishman evidently had what she lacked. It was the way he spoke about the satisfaction he had in Christ that attracted her. 'Jesus said, "If any man thirst, let him come unto me and drink,"' he reiterated, dwelling on the reality of drinking that living water. A conscious desire for the experience was born, not only in Margaret but in her grandmother, and the following year they decided that their trip to Europe should include the Convention to be held in Keswick, in the Lake District of England. The message of total commitment of the life to Christ, and complete confidence in Him to enable His followers to do His will, was what Margaret needed. Discipleship to Jesus Christ meant finding out what He had for her to do, and on her return to Montreal her friends soon observed a change in her. The card parties and dancing she had enjoyed attracted her no more. Instead, she started going to the slums to work with the Salvation Army officers there. She went in and out with them, helping with the distribution of food and clothing, visiting poverty-stricken homes, shepherding people into the Gospel meetings, and trying to dissuade young girls from becoming street-walkers.

It was to these girls and women, the prostitutes, that she was particularly drawn. The shame and degradation of the lives they led repelled her, but she saw beyond that to the girls themselves. 'She made a girl feel that in spite of everything there was something lovable about her,' someone said of her, and naturally that paved the way to the giving of confidences. As she became better acquainted with them she discovered that while some had chosen the life quite deliberately, others had been beguiled or tricked into it. But all of them knew that they were social outcasts now, and that when the hour of their travail came they could expect little help. It was mainly because of her desire to be able to nurse them and the little ones they reluctantly brought into the world that she contrived to take a nursing course in a maternity hospital, although still living with her grandmother. Her family doctor arranged it for her, and later himself taught her the use of simple medical remedies commonly used in his practice. The knowledge she acquired was to prove useful on a much wider scale in the days to come, although the thought of going to China was only latent in her mind at this stage. It was the street girls of Montreal who were primarily claiming her attention, and she had come to know enough about the web in which they could be caught to be prepared to go to unusual lengths to prevent foolish, unwary teenagers from becoming entrapped.

The life she lived was almost a double one. She would go quietly down to the slums, demurely dressed and ready for anything, then return to her grandmother's well-appointed home to take her place in the social circle there. Grandmother Yuile stood behind her in all her activities, however, and some of her friends expressed their willingness to help her in her work. Occasionally she accepted their offers.

'Will you come with me to the Salvation Army Shelter this evening?' she would say. 'I am going to take a girl there tonight. I want you to walk on one side of her, and I on the other, and hold on!' Some of the girl's associates might waylay them and try to get her away. 'We must get there with her safely—we must!' Other more dangerous missions were undertaken with experienced slum workers, or, if need be, she even went alone.

'Terrible scenes she had to face in some of those locked houses,' a friend of hers reported. 'One "keeper" refused to let her in to rescue a girl who had appealed for help. But Margaret got in that night and took the girl. Such courage!'

Getting employment for girls who were prepared to break with the evil life was as difficult as extricating them from it, but Margaret usually managed it. As the years passed she became known as 'our Miss King' to the girls in the red-light district, even those who continued in their drunkenness and degradation. She was the one person they knew who really cared about them, and it drew from them an affection they did not try to disguise. When they heard that she was going to China as a missionary their dismay and grief surprised, even alarmed her. 'But you are our only friend!' they cried. 'Are you really going to leave us?' So genuine was their distress that she began to wonder if she ought to go after all. The girls came to her again and again, tears in their eyes as they clung to her. It was heart-rending for her as well as for them, and when eventually she left for a last lakeside holiday with her own family she was almost exhausted. One of her sisters noticed how tired she was, and asked her about it.

'It was saying goodbye to those girls,' Margaret explained. 'I hadn't realized how much they loved me and depended on me. It made me almost question whether I was right in going away from them.' The inner conflict over leaving the outcast girls who seemed to need her so much was even fiercer than the struggle she had had to part from the grandmother who was so attached to her. The argument that had convinced her she should go was one that appealed to the reason rather than the emotions. Jesus Christ had said, 'Go into all the world and preach the Gospel to every creature.' There were many people doing that in Montreal, and Bibles were available for any who might want them. It was quite different in China. Nearly a quarter of the entire population of the world lived there, with no more preachers to tell them of Christ than in one Canadian city. There could be no question about where the need was greater, and the command to go was implicit. She went to China.

Among other things, it meant a single, not a married life, for already women outnumbered men in the missionary force there, and she knew she was unlikely to meet a life partner. Years earlier she had broken off a friendship that was heading for marriage when she realized the man was not a Christian, and there had never been anyone else who took his place in her affections.

Now there never would be. It left her free to serve her Master without conflicting emotional ties, and this was what she wanted. All the same, those first months in China, separated from her family and the old familiar way of life, were lonely. Her warm, gregarious nature needed human companionship. Throughout her life she was to find it in other woman, and in children. Her great contribution to the work of God in China was among them, and it started soon after she arrived.

Yangchow on the Grand Canal is the city in which the famous Venetian traveller, Marco Polo, had ruled as mandarin for a number of years in the thirteenth century. About two days' journey from Shanghai, it had been chosen by Hudson Taylor as a place well suited for the language school for women missionaries. He and his family and a party of new workers had nearly lost their lives in a riot there twenty and more years before, but that was in the past, and the missionaries in Yangchow had nothing to fear from the inhabitants now. The compound of the language school for thirty or forty young women was also the centre in which Sunday services were held, as well as classes during the week. Here commenced some of the friendships which characterized Margaret's life and played so large a part in it.

The first, surprisingly enough, was with a middle-aged Chinese serving woman, with whom she had long conversations, practising her Chinese. Mrs. Sie admired her diligence in studying the difficult language, and was prepared to give her all the help she could. Other ways of helping soon presented themselves. It became known that

Margaret had some medical knowledge, and there were frequent requests for her services. Off she would go through the narrow, alley-like streets of the city accompanied by Mrs. Sie, whom she described in her letters home as being 'one of the holiest people I ever knew.' Together they would go to the patient's home, and while Margaret administered her medicine Mrs. Sie preached to the onlookers. They teamed up so well that for twenty years, until old age robbed Mrs. Sie of her strength, they were constant companions in evangelism.

Margaret's medical skill opened doors for her into some of the wealthiest homes in the city. Opium had become the scourge of the country, the 'running poison' against which China's rulers had tried in vain to stem the inflow, and it was no unusual thing for a runner to be sent with an urgent request for 'the foreign doctor' to come and save the life of someone who had taken an overdose. She gained quite a reputation as one who was always successful. She depended as much on prayer as on her methods and medicine, but she did not claim to be a miracle worker. She was very practical, and took the wise precaution of sending Mrs. Sie round first to ensure that the case was not already too far gone for treatment.

Once initial contact had been made, she became a welcome guest in several of these homes. One elderly lady whom she was able to cure of a long-standing complaint became very attached to her, and urged her to make free of her home with its twenty or more servants, and one day presented her with a beautiful sedan chair. It was most unsuitable, she said, for the young foreign doctor to be carried to her appointments in mere public transport, hired off the street. She must have her own personal conveyance, and was begged always to use it.

'Live to love, and you will never be lonely' Margaret's mother had written to her very early in her life in China, in response to one of her letters in which she had given expression to her sense of isolation. 'Live in the lives of others, those around you.' She had taken this advice to heart, and was finding it to be true. As she went around the city, visiting the very poor as well as the very rich, she found many sorrowful women, imprisoned by the old Chinese customs that not only bound their feet but fettered their minds and often starved their hearts. The compassion she felt towards them won their affection and ensured her a hearing.

She wanted to be heard. She believed in preaching, proclaiming, explaining, exhorting. It was not enough to heal physical ills and comfort emotional griefs. At best such benefits could only endure for a lifetime. The message she had to deliver was for eternity. She never forgot that.

Her upbringing stood her in good stead, for her Scottish grandmother's courtesy and reserve had prepared her for the leisurely etiquette of the east. She was quick, sometimes impatient, by nature, but she learned to sit smiling and relaxed by the hour, never irked by seemingly trivial talk, or shocked at the polygamy which encouraged wealthy men to take two, three or more wives at a time. She absorbed their culture and came to understand them. It was not sufficient to learn their language if she did not know what they meant by what they said, or inadvertently sat in the wrong seat, or so far forgot herself as to fail to give precedence to a man when it came to walking out of a door. She remained in the language school for some years as a member of staff, and impressed on younger missionaries the importance of knowing the people as well as their tongue. The time came when she knew so well she said, half-laughing, 'I think I've got an oriental heart.'

*　　　　*　　　　*

The Boxer Rebellion of 1900 was a fanatical anti-foreign uprising, supported and encouraged by the all-powerful Dowager Empress. It proved to be a turning-point in the history of China. The secret society of 'Boxers' pledged themselves to the extermination of all foreigners on their soil, and with Imperial backing the movement rapidly gained momentum. In province after province Roman Catholic and Protestant missionaries were forced to flee in peril of their lives, and many were slaughtered. The China Inland Mission lost fifty-eight of its members and twenty-one of their children in the wildfire uprising. Being by this time the largest and most widely spread of the Protestant missions it suffered the most, with so many of its members scattered throughout the interior far from the security of the Treaty Ports.

The number of Chinese Christians who were killed at the same time ran into thousands, but it was the outrage against their own nationals that brought the gunboats of the Western nations into action—and China to its knees. The outcome of it all was that under the enlightened leadership of Li Hung-chang peace was restored, further concessions granted to Westerners living in China, and a change of attitude adopted towards them throughout the nation. No longer could China remain isolated from the rest of the world, the 'middle kingdom' that closed its doors to all outside influences. Diplomacy demanded that the conquerors should be courted, not defied; their skills absorbed, not ignored. It was recognized at last that the Western nations with their formidable fire-belching machines were seeking trade, not territory, and they obviously had skills and instruments and learning that were proving irresistible in the contemporary world.

Parents were eager now to send their children to missionary schools where Western methods of education were adopted, and Yangchow was only one of the many places where such schools were opened. Margaret King was not there at the time, having returned to Canada where she remained longer than she expected, for the sake of her family. By the time she got back to Yangchow to settle there for good, her father, mother and grandmother had all died and China was henceforth her home.

Although her work was still in the field of evangelism, it had been decided that she should live with Emmie Clough, principal of the girls' school. This arrangement met a need they both felt for congenial human companionship which is most easily achieved with another of one's own race and background. Their daily activities were in different spheres, but in the evening there was someone who spoke the same mother tongue with whom to share the evening meal, talk and pray or just sit quietly, reading and writing. Without such a friendship Margaret's life would have been lonely and rather abnormal, but as it was it provided a sort of ballast, steadying the emotions which were often agitated by what she saw and heard as she moved around in the city. The sufferings of the poor, the maimed, the unwanted girl children, the discarded wives, weighed on her. There was little she could do in a practical way to alleviate their lot, although on one occasion at least she saved the life of a baby girl.

Mrs. Sie had come to her in great distress, to tell her of a mother who was planning to do away with her baby daughter—not an unusual thing in China in those days. A daughter was, after all, just another mouth to be fed until a husband could be found, and if the family were poor the easy way out was to ensure that the baby did not live.

Margaret's reaction was immediate. 'Oh, Lord, guide me,' she breathed as she hurried off with Mrs. Sie. By the time she arrived, she had her plan of action. She entered the house and said smilingly.

'I've come to congratulate you.'

'Congratulate?' The woman looked amazed.

'I hear you've had another baby. Do let me see it. Please!'

The baby was not there, she was told, with some embarrassment. It had been taken to its grandmother. But Margaret persisted. She did so want to see the baby, and when at last it was produced, she was almost extravagant in her admiration.

'Oh, how I should like to have this little girl for my own,'

71

she gushed. Then she turned to the woman and said, 'You have other children—won't you give her to me? I'd want you to keep her here and feed her, of course, but I'd pay you for that, and when she's old enough she can come to our school, and I will give her my name.' That child's life was spared, but it did not happen often. As she explained in a letter to a friend in Canada, 'We can help so little, not because we have not the means, but because if we helped our whole time and strength would be taken up with such cases.'

Her home life with Emmie Clough was simple in the extreme. She had the money to build a house of her own on the school compound, and it was the usual practice for missionaries to reside in a separate establishment. The two of them decided against it, however. They knew how much they owed to their own early training, when habits of self-control had been formed and Christian ideals instilled. Character is not built in a day, nor do personalities develop best if children are left to their own devices without the interest, correction and encouragement of their elders. It was not enough to impart knowledge to the pupils in their charge; by precept and practice they should teach them how to live wholesome healthy lives with a readiness to sacrifice self for the good of others. As they talked it over they agreed that they could only do it by living as close to the children as possible. Their dining-room-cum-study therefore opened right on to the school's room, Emmie's bedroom adjoined the dormitory of the older girls, and Margaret had a little reception room built for herself at the end of the dormitory for the younger ones. It had a fireplace and a built-in cupboard, a wide verandah and that is about all. With a few pieces of furniture her private apartment was complete. To get to it she had to cross an open courtyard, often snow-covered in winter, walk through a schoolroom, mount a steep staircase and pass between a double line of little beds from which curious eyes watched every movement.

She might have chosen something a great deal more secluded. It would have been reasonable to insulate herself from the noise and friction of school life at the end of a wearying day of visiting and preaching. Had she done so, she would not have gained the intimate understanding of Chinese life and thought that gave to her preaching such a perceptive edge. It was this which fitted her to make the most of the unprecedented opportunities among young people that opened up in China when the Manchu dynasty eventually came to an end with the revolution that turned China into a Republic.

This happened at the end of 1911, but before that two events had taken place in Margaret's life, each of which was to lead her into a sphere of widening influence. The first was the arrival in China of Dr. Jonathan Goforth, who came there with news of the spiritual revival that was sweeping the churches of Korea and Manchuria. Hundreds of people attended the meetings he held, including Margaret and Mrs. Sie, and as Goforth preached the audience was first hushed, then so deeply moved that for hours people were praying, weeping and confessing sins long hidden until eventually they burst out in praise to God as they became conscious of His forgiveness. The presence of the Holy Spirit was unmistakable. Margaret had never experienced anything like it before, and nor had the others who gathered for those memorable meetings. New depths of penitence were reached as selfishness, hatred, pride, envy were unmasked, and new depths of relief and joy too, as forgiveness was received, together with a fresh empowering. She went back to Yangchow with new power in her own preaching, which was manifested at the very first gathering at which she spoke.

It was a very informal affair, held on a Sunday afternoon, with the pupils and staff of the school grouped in chairs and on the floor of the study, eager to hear about the convention she had attended. The outcome was similar to what had happened at Goforth's much larger meetings. There was the same disturbing consciousness of hitherto unsuspected sin, the same penitence, the tears and the confessions followed by the same sense of freedom and joy. A number of the older girls put their trust in Christ that afternoon, and the atmosphere of the whole school was changed.

News of what was happening in the girls' school at Yangchow soon reached other mission schools, and Margaret was urged to go and lead meetings in them, too. The same thing happened, in varying degrees, in nearly all of the missions she held. Before long she became known as a very effective evangelist, especially among girls of the educated classes.

It was the potential value of these Chinese women to their own nation that impressed her. They had all the intelligence, diligence and staying-power of their race, and she saw what a contribution they could make in society if only they became Christians.

The second significant event occurred when she was taken seriously ill with inflammation of the lungs and was sent to the well-known mountain holiday resort of Kuling to recuperate. Her visit there coincided with the arrival from the U.S.A. of a Dr. W. W. White who, with prophetic insight, saw a new day dawning for China. Opportunities would open up then that must be grasped. There would be a need in the new China for educated women as well as men, who could preach and teach the Word of God. But where, in the whole of the country, was there a seminary in which they could receive the necessary training to equip them for the task? Not one existed.

It was a challenge, but also an inspiration. The establishment of a Bible seminary for well-educated young Chinese women became a dream that must be turned into a reality. Margaret was so clear about her own calling to be an evangelist that she knew she could not take responsibility for it, but she did all in her power to support and encourage those who did.

They needed it. The revolution with Sun Yat Sen at the

helm got off to a good start, with its blossoming of Chinese youth and emancipation from some of the age-old customs that had been the insignia of enslavement to the Manchus. Men shaved off the thin *queues* that had dangled from their crowns, and the habit of binding the feet of baby girls so that they would remain as small as possible began to die out. In the coastal cities, particularly, the change was noticeable. Bright-eyed schoolgirls, their thick black hair bobbed, moved around almost as freely as their brothers. The Youth Movement, brought into being by the dedicated young men and woman students who had backed the revolution, augured well for the new China. Before very long, however, things started to go wrong, with mismanagement, internal strife, and then the rise of the various warlords who fragmented the country, made the roads unsafe, and brought about a state of brigandage unknown under the old regime.

It is not surprising that in the midst of all the turmoil it proved no easy matter to establish anything so progressive as a Bible seminary for women. Applications from suitable students came in slowly, and there were difficulties in obtaining resident staff with the necessary qualifications for Bible teaching. Then someone made the suggestion that suitable people should be invited to come for two or three weeks at a time to give special courses of lectures. Margaret agreed to be one of these, and made so favourable an impression that the principal of the Bible college, who was soon to retire, reported:

. . . what lectures they were! *Intelligible*, for was not the correct use of Chinese one of the passions of Miss King's life; *practical*, for was she not an itinerant missionary with twenty years of experience; *exegetical and theological*, for was she not a Canadian Presbyterian, with the roots of her Bible knowledge extending far back into the kirks where her forebears had worshipped; *fundamental*, for did she not invariably go to the bottom of her subject and dig out the foundation truths which affect Christian faith

75

and character? And lastly, if not chiefly, were they not *inspirational*? For to Miss King the giving of lectures, or a course in Bible study, meant nothing, if the students were not thereby drawn closer to God and filled with a passion to live and witness for Him.

The outcome of those first courses of lectures was that she was urged, unsuccessfully, to join the staff. She could not possibly leave Yangchow, she replied, unless to go to some even more needy place to tell the gospel. Then six months later she received another invitation.

She wrote to her favourite sister,

The committee, representing every mission in all China, want me to become principal of the Nanking Bible School. I am praying about it. I consider it a great honour to be asked. It is a most important work, but whether it is my work or not I do not yet know. Students come from all over China, and one could influence many. I gave the commencement address this year, and it was my Chinese tongue, I fear, that caught the brethren. I wish they had chosen me for some other reason! I may be mistaken, but the Chinese pastors told the committee that that was why they voted for me. The call is unanimous.

In the end she refused it, though she agreed to become a member of the board and to give periodical courses of lectures, as before. God had called her to preach the gospel, and this must come first. So she continued her missions, not only in Yangchow but further afield, travelling sometimes for days on end by boat or wheelbarrow or cart, using whatever means of transport was available.

Many other missionaries were living equally arduous and self-sacrificing lives, for those were days of exceptional opportunity, though of exceptional danger, too, with footpads lurking on the roads and brigands off the beaten track. In one way, however, she was ahead of her time, and that was her eagerness to prepare educated Chinese Christian women for positions of influence. She saw, as few others saw, the need there was for them, and the opportunities they would have in the new China.

From time to time she would take one with her for experience in evangelism. When they travelled with her she expected them to be treated with the same respect as was accorded her. Arriving at one mission station with a young Chinese woman from a highly respected family, she was horrified when she learned that a room had been prepared for her, but not for her companion.

'She can sleep in the hall outside your door,' she was told. It was quite good enough for a young Chinese girl.

'Indeed she cannot!' Miss Margaret King's reaction was immediate and decisive. The very idea! 'She will share the room with me.' And that was that. Her respect and courtesy towards Chinese colleagues grew out of her intimate knowledge of the language and of the sensitive, though well-disguised, feelings of the people. The accusation of imperialistic arrogance, often justly levelled against Westerners, was not levelled against her. As she went off on her missions in response to requests received from over a vast area, she became not only one of the best-known and best-loved missionaries in central China, but one of the very few women to contribute to the discussions of the National Christian Council.

*   *   *

The early years of Margaret King's life in China were overshadowed by the Boxer uprising; her last years by intelligent student propaganda of an anti-foreign nature which spread throughout the nation. Whatever may have been the reasons behind this movement, the result of it was the evacuation of many Westerners, missionaries among them, to the safety of the Treaty Ports in response to consular instructions. This happened on more than one occasion, and took Margaret to Shanghai, into a situation strongly reminiscent of her youthful efforts to rescue girls from prostitution in Montreal.

What she encountered in Shanghai revealed to her horrors of cruelty and suffering beyond anything she had seen or even heard of in Canada. Very few of the girls in the brothels of that eastern port were there through their own fault or choice. Most of them had been bought or kidnapped, and brought to submission by intimidation, even torture. One method employed was to string them up by their thumbs until they were ready to give in to anything rather than endure the excruciating pain any longer. They were then dressed up, their little faces painted and paraded on the streets of the red-light district, perched high on the shoulders of the men who got their money by hiring them out.

There was only one way of escape for them, and that was through a Christian Mission known as the Door of Hope. This had been started some years previously, and was now officially recognised. Any girl who was able to get away from a brothel and appeal for help was handed over to the Door of Hope until her case came up in the courts. If it could be proved that the girl had been illegally detained in the brothel, she could remain in the Christian mission.

There were one hundred and eighty girls there on one of the occasions when Margaret was in Shanghai, 'every one of them with a terrible past, but many now washed and made white in the blood of the Lamb,' she reported.

A number of new girls are in from Yangchow. I wish you could have seen their faces when I began to speak. Some cried, some laughed, and all leaned forward to listen. When I gave the invitation to those who wanted to come to Jesus and be saved, they just crowded up the aisle. I felt as if my heart would break. Patiently, all the rest of the day, I dealt with one and another, hearing their stories. Oh, what stories . . . !

For five days on that occasion she had interview after interview with the girls, whose memories were seared and bruised by what they had suffered, until she almost collapsed with exhaustion, and the string of girls waiting outside her door had to be turned away.

'I hated to leave,' she wrote, and later briefly told of one little girl who had died at the age of thirteen. 'She came in with a terrible disease and just lingered on, sometimes better, sometimes worse. But she died a beautiful Christian. You will be glad to know,' she added, her outraged sense of justice somewhat appeased, 'that, owing to the fight these ladies put up to rescue the child, her owner was deported.' She would gladly have thrown in her lot with the courageous workers of the Door of Hope, but her call to evangelism remained as strong as ever, and when things had quietened down she returned to Yangchow and her preaching missions in the high schools and colleges to which she was frequently invited.

Her vision for the girls there always went beyond the initial step of leading them to personal faith in Christ. She told them that there was now a work they could do for Christ in their own country, and that there was a place where they could be trained to do it—the Nanking Bible School. (It later became well known as the Kiangwan Bible Seminary of Shanghai.) Her promotion work proved very effective.

'Soon there began to appear in the student body young women who had dedicated their lives in some meeting or mission led by Miss King,' the principal reported. 'The number grew with the years, and one day I was astonished to see how many Presbyterians, Baptists, Methodists and girls of other communions came running to meet this China Inland Mission missionary. Evidently it was she who had helped them into the surrendered life and directed them into the Bible School.'

She continued her work and manner of life right up to the end. Yangchow on the Grand Canal had been her home from the time she first arrived in China, and it was here that she died, as the 1930s dawned. It had been a happy Christmas for her, surrounded by friends and colleagues, missionary and Chinese, along with her adopted Chinese daughter and her family. Margaret was unusually tired after the celebrations—she could not understand why. Then pneumonia set in.

'Am I dying?' she asked. 'Tell me the truth. I must know.' When she knew she was silent for a moment or two, then said rather regretfully,

'I should like to do more for Him down here. My service has been so poor and little ...' Then her face became radiant, as though she could see something beyond. Asked what it was, she whispered, 'Heaven! Heaven!'

And so the pilgrimage ended.

Now, dear friends, some of you have been following me these past fifteen years with your prayers and gifts for these women's evangelistic missions in different provinces. God certainly opened this larger field of service to me, and I have accepted and visited all the provinces where I have been invited . . .

I feel now very clearly this door is closing to me. He may be calling others, Chinese or foreigners to this work, younger ones with better and newer methods. My station has loaned me for this work for fifteen years, and has always sent me forth with joy and received me home again with joy, and now it is finished: they invite me to return and be one of the active members of the station again at Hwailu. I feel this is of God, and I have accepted it.

Perhaps it may interest you to know these past fifteen years I have visited fifteen provinces, held 183 missions, and those going through the enquiry rooms showing their desire of wanting to follow Jesus Christ have been 5,342 women and girls.

Written by Jessie Gregg to her friends in 1926.

Praise God, I was not disobedient to the heavenly vision; while the door was open, I entered. Today it would be quite impossible to enter many of those doors.

Written at the close of her missionary career, in an article entitled These Forty Years, *in 1937.*

4. Unlikely Revivalist

Jessie Gregg

Jessie Gregg was a buoyant, sometimes quite a boisterous person, with a childlike directness and an urge to get moving. Since she had had a little nursing experience when at the age of twenty-two she went into the China Inland Mission's training home for women, and since she was very certain that God had called her to go to China, she expected to be sent off forthwith. What was there to hinder her going? She found it very irksome, to say the least, to receive a gentle but firm negative reply to her constant question, 'Shall I see the Council next time they meet?'

There was something about the staff of the training home that made her feel uncomfortable and out of place, and she did not like it. Then she began to realize that the 'something' was the Holy Spirit. The staff spoke of Him reverently yet lovingly, as though He were a living Person, not just a vague influence as she had thought. They spoke about Him filling them, guiding and controlling them. They must be very special, holy people, she thought, but she was not like that. She was not special, and she did not feel at all holy, so how could she expect Him to fill her? She wished she could just walk out and buy a ticket and go home, but she knew she couldn't. She must stick it out somehow.

Then one day she saw a stream of water gushing out of an old lead pipe. It was a battered, bent, rusty old pipe, but that did not make any difference to the water. It gushed out through that open channel, clear and sparkling, and in a flash the truth dawned. Jesus said, *'He that believeth on me, as the scripture hath said, out of his belly shall flow rivers of living water.'* The pipe was simply a channel. All that was required of it was that it should be available and that there should be no obstruction in it—then the water would flow.

'O God, make me like this old lead pipe!' she prayed. 'Let Thy Holy Spirit fill me and flow out to others, like the water through this pipe.' She little knew to what a degree that prayer was to be answered.

After the usual period of two years' training she went to China, spent six months in the women's language school at Yangchow, and then was sent up to the city of Hwailu in the northern province of Hopeh. The skies are usually blue in north China, and in the summer the days are hot, but in the winter the nights are very, very cold. It was not the weather that bothered her, however. It was the language. Smallpox had broken out in the language school while she was there, and she had been called on to do some very heavy nursing, which had hindered her study. When she arrived at Hwailu she discovered, to her dismay, that none of the Chinese could understand what she was trying to say.

However, there was an old lady living on the mission compound who felt very much for this inarticulate young foreigner, and who prayed for her daily, explaining to the Lord that there was a missionary who had come, but who could not talk. She was twenty-five years old, lived in the west room of the courtyard, and her tongue was so stiff that she couldn't get it round Chinese words. Would He therefore kindly give her the *oil* of the Holy Spirit to loosen her tongue, so that she could speak clearly.

The old lady's prayer was answered. Jessie passed all the required language exams without difficulty or delay, and by the time the year 1900 dawned she had a thoroughly good understanding of what was being voiced in that centre of news, views and rumours: the market.

The news was depressing, and had been for several months. The harvest had failed, due to lack of rain. The price of grain had gone up. The price of grain had gone up again. The price of grain was going up and up.

The views on the subject began to sound an ominous note when it was whispered that the presence of foreigners on Chinese soil was the cause of the drought, and that the gods were angry.

The rumours arising out of this were alarming, especially when it was learned that the society known as the Boxers were bent on the extermination of foreigners, and were already on the rampage to the north of Hwailu. But when the rumours crystallized into facts, and it was known that the railway had been destroyed, the engineers attacked, and that communication with the outside world was cut off, except by telegram, then the little groups of missionaries scattered throughout the vast area began to realize that their lives were in imminent danger.

The news reached Jessie Gregg and her colleagues, Mr. and Mrs. C. H. S. Green, at the beginning of June. After a month of increasing tension, during which the mission compound was burgled at night on several occasions, they heard that the missionaries in a neighbouring city had been killed and the premises destroyed, and that the Governor of Shansi, known to be in sympathy with the Boxers, was advancing on Hwailu with an armed force. Friends and well-wishers came secretly, urging them to hide. Then a traveller arrived from a neighbouring city saying that the missionaries there had applied in vain for protection in the Yamen, and had fled into the countryside. A missionary in another city had been robbed, while the mission premises of yet another had been destroyed and looted. Hard on the heels of this harbinger of bad news came another, from a different direction, but with a similar story. Within a couple of hours on that momentous day, 5 July 1900, they learned that their nearest mission centres to the north, south, east and west had all been attacked, and that their colleagues either had been killed or were in hiding.

There was nothing else for it—they must flee. Before

daybreak the next day they were secreted in one room in a temple some miles outside the city.

The fact that Jessie and the Green family lived through the next few months at all is due entirely to the amazing courage and loyalty of Chinese who befriended them, to a mysterious interweaving of events which they had no hesitation in acknowledging as God's overruling, and to their own inner fortitude. They were in an incredibly perplexing situation, and so were the Chinese authorities. The Boxers were now officially recognized by the powerful Dowager Empress and her party. 'Death to the foreign devils!' was their cry, curved swords flashing defiance, international treaties scorned. Moderate voices in high places reasoned that since the foreigners' medicine, and the foreigners' technology, and above all the foreigners' war machines were proving vastly superior to those of the Chinese, the wisest course was to come to terms with the facts and act accordingly. China could no longer stand aloof from the rest of the world: if isolation would give way to co-operation, she could still retain her sovereignty. But the moderate voices were being silenced, and the mandarins in their Yamens, with their age-old obligation to uphold law and order, were in a dilemma. They knew they ought to protect the foreigners who had come legally to reside in their country, but with the Boxers carrying all before them, they were afraid to do so. In the northern provinces, where the Boxers were most powerful, the best that the mandarins could do was to send the foreigners away with a few hundred Chinese *cash*, as quickly as possible, for some other mandarin to deal with. Anything to get rid of them. The worst they could do was to hand them over to the Boxers, and since anyone suspected of being in sympathy with the foreigners was likely to be summarily dealt with (thousands of Chinese lost their lives for this reason) it is not surprising that in some cases that is what happened.

And so, for nearly four months, Jessie and Mr. and Mrs. Green, with their two small children, were homeless fugitives in inland China. A friendly temple keeper provided them with refuge for six days, then when their whereabouts was reported they were smuggled into the isolated home of a farmer. They were there for a month, not daring to move out of their room until darkness had fallen, their servants coming from the city secretly to bring news and provisions. Then, knowing that once more the Boxers were on their track, they retreated into a damp little cave, and while they were there Jessie had one of the outstanding spiritual experiences of her life. It was only a matter of minutes before they would be discovered, but in that time words came into her mind, clear, strong and steadying.

'A thousand shall fall at thy side, and ten thousand at thy right hand, but it shall not come nigh thee.'

The consciousness of His presence stilled every fear for her that terrible day. The Boxers found them. Mr Green was shot in the head, their spectacles, watches, rings were stripped from them, then they were pushed, dishevelled and bleeding, down the mountain, along the road, and back into the city. Crowds lined the streets watching them with silent sympathy, and as they stumbled along Jessie caught sight of the anguished face of Mrs. Liu, one of their servants. The woman was making no effort to disguise her grief and horror at what was happening to them and Jessie, conscious still of the Voice she had heard in the cave, called out to her,

'We are not afraid! God is with us!' The people of Hwailu remembered that.

They were taken to the Yamen that night. Then began the period of exposure. For five weeks they had been hidden, scarcely daring to speak for fear of being discovered. Now that was over, and there was no more privacy. Early next day they were put on a springless cart to be sent to the next city, but the mandarin there only wanted to be rid of them, so on they went, stared at by all who passed them. They spent most of the night in the Yamen prison, along with six chained men, and early next morning were put on the cart again. Back and forth they went, bumped and jolted, the sun beating down on them; it seemed endless. Bruised and aching, thirsty, drooping, they were a spectacle for men and angels.

They thought deliverance was coming to them when, at one place, they were put on a boat and told they were being sent to Tientsin, 'from where you can return to your own country.' But some distance down river, in an isolated spot, they were put ashore.

'The Boxers told us to kill you when we got you in a quiet place,' the boatmen said. 'But we cannot commit that sin. You can get off here and we'll leave you. You'll have to fend for yourselves.' And they rowed away, leaving the bewildered little group, laden with their few remaining possessions, to hide in the rushes and try to pray and decide what to do.

It was not easy to do either. Prayer had been instinctive and persistent all the time until now, but sitting on their bedding, alone in a strange place where they knew no one, afraid to show themselves and appeal for help, they felt numbed. The hours passed slowly. They were waiting for nightfall, when they hoped they might quietly emerge and find a boatman willing to take them towards Tientsin, and as they crouched among the reeds the strangest thought became lodged in Jessie's mind. She could not account for it.

'Has the Lord been speaking to you?' Mr. Green asked his wife, conscious of his need of encouragement.

'I still have the same text as before,' she replied. '"Delivering thee from the people . . . unto whom now I send thee."' It seemed so unlikely of fulfilment now, and yet, as they reminded themselves, they had already been delivered three or four times from what had seemed like certain death. That they were still alive at all, that the boatmen had not killed them as ordered, was an evidence of deliverance.

'And what has the Lord been saying to you?' Mr. Green asked Jessie.

But Jessie had no text to give him. Instead—

'I've been waiting all day for a little bird to bring us a letter,' she answered, and in spite of themselves they had to laugh. 'A little bird to bring us a letter'! In the circumstances, could any expectation be more ludicrous? Jessie laughed too, but the thought of a letter persisted.

They emerged at nightfall and met a youth who seemed ready to befriend them, but instead he sent word to the Boxers, and once more they were surrounded. Now came the worst time of all. They were pummelled, beaten to the ground, trussed up like animals, then Jessie was dragged by the hair to a kneeling position, her head banged down on a stone table, and a voice yelled,

'Who will strike?'

So this was the end. Never had she known such calm. In a moment it would all be over, and she would be forever with the Lord.

But no sword struck. Instead, other voices were raised. 'No. Take them to headquarters.' She was pushed down into the mud, and beaten again and again with the backs of swords and handles of spears.

'As blow after blow fell upon her no sound escaped her lips, only a long, deep sigh,' said Mr. Green afterwards. He was lying beside her, receiving the same treatment, his wife also bound hand and foot some distance away. The terrified shrieks of the children had ceased, and it was almost with a sense of relief that he thought they must be dead, and out of the horror they could not understand.

Now spears were brought into action as poles. Jessie was slung by an arm and a leg over one of them and carried along the road to the temple being used as headquarters, where she was dumped on the ground, Mr. and Mrs. Green beside her. Then they heard again the cries of the children, who had been taken into a house, and since they could not be pacified they were let go, and came tottering on their little bare feet to sink down beside their mother and sob themselves to sleep.

The three grown-ups did not sleep, though. As they huddled together, still bound, in the darkness, they agreed that they had known the greatest peace they had ever experienced when they thought they were going to die. They had not the strength to say much or to pray long, but deep, deep thoughts of Christ's pathway to Calvary filled their minds, and as they lay there wet, aching and muddy, they murmured, 'It's all for Jesus' sake . . .'

*   *   *

They were kept for a week on the floor of the main hall of the temple, unwashed, guarded by five or six soldiers, and pestered from morning to night by curious sightseers who thronged in to look at them and ask idle questions. Coarse food was brought morning and evening, but it was so indigestible the children got diarrhoea (not for the first time), as did Mrs. Green. Jessie, the strongest member of the party now, really knew what it was to suffer from sheer hunger. The flies, the vermin, the stench, the humiliation, the tension of uncertainty and the terror of the children continued to make that week one of the worst of their experience, though there were moments when the kindness of some of the people in giving tasty food to the children eased their strain. It was further alleviated when Jessie's plea to be allowed to go to the river to wash clothes was at last granted, and from time to time, accompanied by an armed guard, she managed to wash and rub away the worst of the filth and mud. They all had only what clothes they stood up in, so there was a careful rearrangement of garments to wear, and garments to wash, each time she went out, leaving the half-naked family crouching under the scanty bedding.

They had to snatch what sleep they could during the day, for the discomforts of the night were intensified by the rats, and at midday worshippers and sightseers left the temple comparatively empty. Early one afternoon Jessie was taking advantage of Mr. Green's offer to fan off the flies while she and the others slept, when she was awakened suddenly and saw him beckon her and his wife to look at a crumpled piece of paper he was smoothing out with his hand.

'A man came and threw this in. Look at it!' he whispered excitedly, glancing cautiously at the sleeping guard. Together they leaned forward and read with amazement the words that had been written in a clear strong hand.

'Don't be afraid, for Chinese robbers nearly all have been killed by both Chinese and foreign soldiers. Peking and Tientsin belong to Europeans. Now I will go to Tientsin and tell your armies to protect you. You may tear this into pieces when you have seen.'

Jessie held her breath, then looked at the other two, half laughing, half crying.

'I told you so,' she said. 'That day we were hiding by the river. A little bird with a letter for us. This is it.'

They never met the man who sent them that reassuring message of hope, and they had several more weeks of captivity to live through, and the grief of seeing little five-year-old Vera die of dysentery, before they finally reached Tientsin at the end of October. They had touched bottom in hardship and degradation in that temple, however, and gradually their circumstances improved, even before the arrival of French and English forces brought them relief. They later learned that 'the little bird with the letter' who had come so silently and mysteriously was a wealthy Chinese businessman who had fled from Tientsin at the time when it was captured by the allied forces, and that it was largely due to his wise counsel that their lives had been spared when they were imprisoned in the temple, at the apparent mercy of the Boxers. If he had fled to some other city than the one they happened to be in, their story might have had a different ending. They had, indeed, been given up for dead, after rumours from several sources asserted that the Boxers had killed them by the river.

In all, 117 Protestant missionaries were killed during the

Boxer uprising, fifty-eight of them members of the China Inland Mission. When Jessie thought it over afterwards, remembering how time and time again the Boxers had inexplicably stopped short at killing her, she knew she had been saved out of it all for a purpose. She had experienced her baptism of suffering. Now she was ready for her life's work. She was just thirty years of age when, in 1901, after a furlough in England, she returned to China and with Mr. and Mrs. Green went straight back to Hwailu.

*   *   *

They made a good team. They had been through so much together, theirs was to be a loyal partnership all the years they spent in China. Mr. and Mrs. Green had depended a great deal on Jessie during the Boxer troubles, for without the sturdy help of their younger companion they and the children would have suffered even more than they did. Mr. Green was weakened through loss of blood, and in pain with many pellets imbedded in his flesh from the gun shot that had wounded him, amd Mrs. Green had never been physically strong. 'I was turned down by the Council on health grounds,' she told Jessie. 'I was heartbroken, but Mrs. Benjamin Broomhall encouraged me. She advised me to go home, build up my strength with plenty of rest and good food, and to apply again. I did, and they accepted me. I'd never have got to China if it had not been for her.' The marvel was that she had survived those terrible months at all.

Now the three of them were back again in Hwailu, ready to resume their previous roles, Mr. Green in charge of the work generally, gentle Mrs. Green the homemaker and leader of women's classes in the city, and Jessie, hearty and strong, the country worker.

She spent most of her time living in Chinese homes, and it was here that she gained the intimate knowledge of idiom and custom, of hidden evils and secret alliances, that was to make her such an effective evangelist in years to come. Off she would go with her woman servant, dressed in Chinese trousers and jacket, to some home in a village or town where a friendly invitation had been given to her to come and stay, and to 'preach the way'. Her single status was no disadvantage, for it placed her in Chinese minds in the special category of 'holy women', devotees of their religion, initiated into its mysteries, and distinct from the common run of humanity. The fact that she was a young, healthy and attractive woman travelling unescorted in a country where such freedom was unknown aroused no suspicion, provoked no adverse comments. She was different. She was a foreigner for one thing, and she was a 'holy woman' for another. Even men were prepared to give her a hearing, although she made it plain that she had come to teach women. Men, she pointed out, had plenty of opportunity to hear the Word of God. Mr. Green or evangelists from the city church would readily come to teach and to preach to them, and they could go in to Hwailu any time they liked to hear more. For the women it was not the same. They weren't free to come and go as they would. It was for them she had come, and it was to them she addressed herself, sitting with them in their courtyards as they picked over grain, spun cotton thread, or made quilts and garments; going with them into their dark, smoke-blackened kitchens to watch them cook; laboriously and patiently teaching them to read, to sing, to pray.

As the years passed, it was Jessie who in the main did the pioneering work in a neighbourhood which proved singularly responsive. The cruel depredations of the Boxers, and the subsequent victories of the allied forces had ushered in a new era of tolerant, even eager acceptance of Western innovations, and in places there was almost a mass movement towards Christianity. It was heartening in some ways, though disturbing in others, when people who appeared to be genuine believers were baptized and received as church members, only to reveal later that ulterior motives had moved them, rather than genuine conviction. Nevertheless, the gospel was proclaimed far and wide, and little groups of believers with a Chinese evangelist were established in six cities which Jessie could claim to have opened.

She herself was developing into an outstandingly effective preacher. She was a born story-teller, with a sense of the dramatic and a simplicity of speech that was never cluttered with non-essentials. Her intimate knowledge of Chinese life enabled her to unmask wrongdoing with an accuracy that left her hearers speechless as she brought home to them the laws of God that they had broken. When she went on to tell of the Son of God who on the cross had taken the punishment due to them, there were times when women broke down in tears—tears of penitence followed by tears of joy at the relief of having received forgiveness. The change in their lives after that was evidence of the change that had taken place in their hearts. Reports of what was happening among women in Hwailu began to seep through to missionaries in other centres. 'I wish Miss Gregg could come and work here,' they said. The revelation that had come to her in her training days, when she saw water gushing from a battered, rusty pipe, was to be fulfilled in greater measure than ever she had anticipated. She was destined to launch out into a work no other woman had ever done in China.

It started when an invitation came to her from Hwochow, a large city in a neighbouring province. Here a Christian school for girls had been established, as well as a flourishing church with a number of outstations in the countryside. The missionaries there had both vision and enterprise, and it was they who sent an unusual request. Would Miss Jessie Gregg come and speak at a five days' mission for women only, to which women from the outstations would be invited. It had never been attempted before, but they believed the time was ripe to try it now.

An evangelistic mission for women? A residential mission lasting for five days? It seemed a preposterous idea in a country where woman's place was indisputably in the home and nowhere else. Anyone knowing China would realize how impossible it was. A woman, an ordinary country woman, to go away from home for five whole days, to live on a mission compound merely for the purpose of listening to a preacher? Who would do the cooking at home, feed the animals, look after the children and 'watch the gate'?

But this instinctive reaction against the suggestion had been overcome, so Miss Mildred Cable, Principal of the girl's school in Hwochow, was able to assure Miss Gregg. The church elders had begun to recognize their responsibility towards their illiterate wives, and to realize that home as well as church would be a better place if the women had an intelligent faith in Christ, and were instructed in His ways. So with the moral support of the church elders the missionaries in Hwochow were asking Miss Gregg if she would come as speaker at a mission for women—the first of its kind ever to be held in China.

She accepted the invitation and went. Thorough preparations had been made, with rooms on the compound cleared to accommodate women by the score, enormous cooking pots, piles of grain, jars of oil stood ready in the kitchens, benches enough for a congregation of five hundred in the large new chapel. The missionaries, Bible women and older schoolgirls had been at it for several days with special classes and prayer meetings, and all were agog with mingled expectation and apprehension.

The overriding question at that stage was whether the country women from the outstations would actually come, or whether at the last minute their courage would fail, or their mothers-in-law forbid them to leave, or their husbands change their minds. Spirits were beginning to flag an evening or two before the mission was due to commence, when sounds from the front courtyard heralded the arrival of a cartload of women—then another—then another. When thirteen cartloads had been accounted for, and the excited occupants, each complete with bedding roll and face basin, towel and wooden comb, had been settled down for the night, spirits had risen noticeably. The next day more arrivals, this time women on donkeys including one string of twenty, gave assurance that numerically at any rate the mission was already a success.

'The new chapel was filled with between four and five hundred women and girls. Not a man in the place! All women!' said Jessie afterwards. 'The sight made one's heart leap with thanksgiving that we had at last got hold of the women of China, and that the women were coming into the fold of Jesus Christ.'

On the third or fourth day of the mission something happened which set the seal on Jessie's ministry and established her calling. The subject of her address was the harvest, and she was teaching her audience to learn a verse of scripture.

'Whose fan is in his hand, and he will thoroughly purge his floor, and gather his wheat into the garner, but he will burn up the chaff with unquenchable fire.' As they repeated it time and time again, a sense of awe stole over the gathering, and Jessie, a prayer in her heart, said suddenly,

'You know, in this meeting this afternoon there are only two kinds of people.' The solemnity of what she was saying added the note of deep emotion to her voice as she continued with typical directness,

'Just two kinds of people—the chaff and the wheat. That's all. If you are not the chaff you are the wheat. If you are not the wheat, then you are the chaff. Which are you?'

It was a very simple thing to say, but the timing was perfect. The effect was very similar to that described in the book of the Acts, when Peter preached at Pentecost.

'. . . the Holy Spirit fell upon that meeting. A mighty wave of conviction swept over the gathering, and over ninety women decided for Christ that afternoon.' At the end of the mission, when an opportunity was given for anyone who wanted to speak, 225 women and girls stood up and told briefly of their decision to follow Him. Miss Mildred Cable, one not given to exaggeration or effusive enthusiasm, wrote afterwards, 'It has been a wonderful and never-to-be-forgotten time.' Then she added, 'I am impressed in being with Miss Gregg again during these days with the fact that in the diversities of gifts bestowed by the Spirit, she has manifestly been given that of the *evangelist*. I am thankful this has been recognized, and that some of our stations are being privileged to have a visit from her.'

This was the apparent beginning of Jessie's wider ministry, but in reality it had started much earlier. As she herself expressed it, 'a great burden for souls was laid upon my heart, and I cried, "Give me children or I die."' The travail of soul through which she passed was something she could not communicate to others, but it was by no easy apprenticeship that she had been prepared for her ministry. Nor was the way ahead smooth and unhindered. Once more a political upheaval disrupted plans, as the deaths first of the Dowager Empress, then of the weak young Emperor, saw the end of the Manchu dynasty and the ushering in of the Republic. When things had settled down, however, she was back again in Hwailu.

For nearly fifteen years after that her life was one of almost ceaseless travel as she went from province to province holding evangelistic campaigns for women. The same sort of results were evident everywhere she went, with women flocking to hear her, and many of them confessing long-hidden sins, then receiving the forgiveness promised through faith in Christ Jesus.

'I never heard anything like it in China,' reported one missionary, while another wrote,

The women are won by Miss Gregg's personality and manner, and the message of the cross, grand in the simplicity and clearness with which it is delivered, seems mighty through the Holy Spirit's working. She left us yesterday, and I have never seen in China anything like the love the women showed as they watched, in the distance, the very last glimpse of the sedan bearing the Lord's messenger on her way . . .

She was in constant demand. Her name became almost a household word as members of other missionary societies heard reports of what was happening, and begged the privilege of a visit from her to their centres also. The C.I.M. had no work in Manchuria, but she spent nearly a year there in response to such requests.

During the fifteen years which marked the peak of her ministry she travelled in thirteen provinces, covering about 20,000 miles, 'a distance of more than once round the world,' as she explained when on deputation work in England. She had a head for figures, and kept accurate reports of her journeyings and campaigns which she used to good effect when speaking. If the women she had travelled so widely to reach could all have been congregated together, they would have filled the Albert Hall nine times. She knew of over five thousand women and girls who had been converted as a result of those meetings, and that in many places a new impetus had been given to evangelistic work among women. In all those fifteen years she had been able to fulfil every engagement but one. On that occasion she arrived on time, but collapsed on the doorstep with typhoid fever. All the same, she took a lively interest in what happened. Someone else stepped into her place at the last minute, and Jessie, lying in her bedroom which was right over the chapel, with only a wooden partition between her and the congregation, listened eagerly to all that went on.

'I heard Miss Flinkman plead with those women she knew so well unreservedly to give themselves to the Lord Jesus Christ. On the first day of the mission twenty-seven of those women decided for Him,' she reported triumphantly afterwards, adding wryly, 'As you can imagine, my temperature went up that night!'

In her speaking she referred only lightly to what it had all involved for her personally—the long, arduous journeys, sometimes in crowded trains and boats, more often over lonely roads and paths, by mule-back, wheelbarrow, or springless carts, exposed to the weather, travelling for days on end, in cold as well as in heat. Some of those journeys took her through brigand-infested areas, and on one occasion, travelling with a young Finnish missionary, they were suddenly accosted by armed men who looked as though they would stop at nothing. Jessie, with her usual resourcefulness, whipped off her hat, disclosing her grey hair. She knew the Chinese respect for age, and it stood her in good stead that day. To their credit, the men stood back and allowed her and her companion to pass by unmolested. But she knew the dangers to which she was exposed as she travelled some of those roads. It was brought home to her very forcibly shortly afterwards, when she learned that brigands had broken into the town where that young Finnish missionary was living and had killed her, along with others, outright.

It was when travelling alone along one such isolated stretch of road, in the dead of winter, that she had an experience which crowned her life, and which she never forgot. It transformed for her all the years ahead. She was cold, and in order to get her circulation quickened decided to walk for a while. She was feeling rather depressed. The loneliness of being without a permanent companion to relieve the monotony of the constant travelling weighed on her. She would not yield to self-pity, of course, so she forced herself to sing aloud as she trudged on through the snow.

> I need Thee, oh, I need Thee,
> Every hour I need Thee,
> Oh bless me now, my Saviour,
> I come to Thee . . .

The words were familiar, and she sang almost automatically though it was a prayer, when suddenly she became aware of a Presence beside her as she walked, and of a

Voice taking up the words she was singing. And the words she heard as she walked on in a sort of trance-like ecstasy illuminated all her life of service with an unspeakable glory, for she heard her Master singing,

> I need thee, oh, I need thee,
> Every hour I need thee . . .

So conscious was she of His Presence that she turned instinctively to look at Him. 'He just showed me His hands and His feet and was gone,' she said afterwards, but the memory and the message remained. She needed Him—oh, how she needed Him! But, wonder of wonders—He needed her. To reach those women of China, He needed her.

*   *   *

Jessie Gregg's missions for women ceased as clearly and distinctively as they had begun. While she was home on furlough in 1928 it was discovered that she was suffering from diabetes. It was doubtful for a time if she would be allowed to return to China at all, but with careful attention to diet and a quieter life it was decided she could do so. She went back to Hwailu, which had always been her home in China, and for seven years lived in a town some twenty miles away, once more an ordinary, upcountry missionary on whom the limelight no longer shone. Her mantle had passed to others and names like Marie Monsen, Anna Christensen and Miss Tippet took the place of Jessie Gregg. She returned to England, and in 1942 she died, cheerful and buoyant to the end. As Mildred Cable, who visited her shortly before she died, reported, 'She is waiting for the call, looking forward with utter joy for a sight of the King in His beauty.'

I went to the Scotch Kirk this evening, in a beautiful, wealthy, comfortable church with a splendid choir, just like a lovely home church. We came back past the big pagoda, twinkling in the moonlight—and past hundreds of yellow-robed Buddhist priests, and my heart felt heavy. It must be very discouraging for the Lord. He must think that we might have done better.

Written in a letter by Dr. Jessie McDonald from Rangoon, Burma, in 1941, on her way to pioneer medical work in the mountains of south-west China.

5. Pushed To the Front Line

Dr. Jessie McDonald

No one likes to be seen crying in a railway carriage, certainly not shy seventeen-year-old girls leaving home for the first time. Jessie McDonald was buoyed up with excitement and waved gaily to her parents and sister as the train pulled out of Vancouver station, but when she settled back in her seat and saw only complete strangers around her, she suddenly felt frightened. She was alone. Quite alone. The thought came over her like a dark fog, and it was then that she realized she was going to cry. She had just sufficient presence of mind to see that the window was open, and that if she leaned out it would appear that she was admiring the scenery, and no one would see her tears. Quickly she thrust her head out, clutched her handkerchief and sobbed.

She sobbed for quite a long time, until in the distance she saw the mountains, and her knowledge of the Psalms came to her aid. 'Unto the hills will I lift up my longing eyes,' she repeated to herself, and if the familiar lines did not immediately stay her tears, they brought a measure of comfort. All the same, she kept on leaning out of the window.

Eventually the attendant came along to make up the sleeping berths, so she had to move to take a seat. She did so as unobtrusively as possible, and hoped that the young man sitting opposite would not notice that she had been crying. However, he was a kind young man, and he could not fail to see that her nose was pink, and her eyes wet and swollen.

'Are you going to school?' he enquired sympathetically. Jessie was too woebegone to correct him.

'No,' she replied. 'To university. Toronto University.'

'Oh!' The young man saw he had made a mistake, and hurried on to cover it up. 'Have you got any friends in Toronto?'

'Yes. Dr. Wallace, the minister of Bluer Street Presbyterian Church is a cousin of my mother's.'

'Why, his son is a friend of mine—in the same class,' exclaimed the young man. 'You'll love university,' he continued cheerfully. 'You'll be quite free. No one to notice if you skip classes. It's all up to you whether you take exams or not, pass or not! No one to keep track of you . . .'

Jessie's heart sank. No one! It was the very thought that was oppressing her. All through the night she lay awake in her berth as the train thundered on, and as dawn came she watched the changing panorama from the Rocky Mountains to the prairies, then the lake country with the brilliant rich colour of the maples. No one! It was very beautiful, she thought, but . . .

And when she arrived at Toronto, dismounted from the train and waited for the cousin who was to come and meet her, no one came. No one! She stood there terror-stricken. But the kind young man had his eye on her, and after a time he said,

'Let's not wait any longer. I'll hire a cab and take you to the door.' When they arrived it was to find that Jessie had been expected, but not until the next day. There were welcomes, explanations and thanks all round, the kind young man departed, and Jessie was so overwhelmed with joy and relief at having arrived safely that she did not know whether to laugh or to cry. She never forgot the emotional upheaval of what was for her the first step of the path that would lead her to China.

There had been no other objective for her but China since she was about seven, when she had gone to the church where her mother helped Chinese immigrants by teaching them English; after listening for a while she said that she wanted to have a Chinese pupil, too. Initial surprise at the suggestion had given way to the realization that however limited might be a child's knowledge of English, it was greater than that of a Chinese who knew none at all. She could read simple books, and the Chinese liked children because, as they explained, they spoke clearly. So a man had become her pupil, and the serious minded little seven-year-old had got on very well until she discovered that he did not understand who Jesus was, and what was meant by praying. Such ignorance amazed her, and she told her mother about it.

'Well, dear, he comes from a country called China, and they've never heard about Jesus there,' she had been told. The explanation had not satisfied her. It had merely led on to another question.

'Then why didn't you go and tell them?' she had demanded. Further explanations had plunged her into deep thought which led to a decision from which she never budged.

'When I get big, I'm going to China.' Eventually everyone had to take her seriously.

The McDonald home was frequently visited by missionaries and one arrived one day wearing a tall black hat and a very old-fashioned black suit which had been with him all the way to the New Hebrides and back again. His manners were courtly, his prayers profound, but his life seemed to have been so hard that Jessie was discouraged. She could never be a missionary like him, pioneering, preaching, plunging into the unknown, braving all sorts of dangers and still battling on. She had not realized missionary work was like that. She had thought it was just a matter of going to another country, learning the language, then sitting and teaching people to read the Bible and explaining to them about Jesus. If it involved preaching in the open air, facing fierce men bent on knifing her, cutting her way through jungles and wrestling with the unseen powers of darkness,

105

she began to wonder if she could make the grade. Then the missionary said something that flashed like a torch through the gathering blackness, lighting a path along which she saw that she could tread.

'What we need desperately is a doctor,' he said. There was so much physical suffering that could be alleviated, and to do it was such a wonderful way to demonstrate the love of God. Medical missionaries were in the vanguard of evangelism in backward countries.

A medical missionary. This was it! Jessie decided that she couldn't be the pioneering sort of missionary, but she could be a doctor. She would go as a missionary doctor to China. And so it came about that she entered the medical school at Toronto University in 1905, a very youthful-looking seventeen-year-old, and a girl at that.

It was quite a new thing for women to study medicine in Canada, though the door for them had opened much earlier in the U.S.A. There were only four other young women in Jessie's class; all the rest were confident young males, and there seemed to be scores of them.

She was still feeling out of her depth when she received an invitation extended to all the Freshmen, to attend a play in a theatre. This put her in a very difficult position. She had never been to a play in a theatre in her life. To do so was considered worldly in the circle where her family moved, and the thought of how her parents would feel, if they knew she had been to one, filled her with dismay. It outweighed the embarrassment of being the only one in her class to refuse the invitation. 'I don't think I'll go, thank you,' she said. But why not? Everyone goes! The inevitable reaction meant explaining rather feebly why she didn't go to theatres or dances, or anything like that. She felt very foolish at first, but afterwards she was glad she had settled the matter right at the start. It put her into the category where she belonged, and preserved her from fruitless distractions.

There was a very active branch of the Student Volunteer Movement in the university, and she promptly enrolled as

106

a member. 'The evangelization of the world in this generation' was its motto, and it challenged her. She had often privately condemned former generations of Christians for their slackness in carrying the gospel to the ends of the earth. Now she concluded that each generation was responsible for those of its own time, hers as much as those that had gone before. The generation to which she belonged must answer for itself. It put her on her mettle, and the words of a missionary from China imprinted themselves on her mind. 'One million Chinese die every month without having once heard the gospel.' She wondered sometimes how many Chinese she was responsible for.

She had thrown in her lot with the evangelical minority, and it was well that she had done so, for her faith was assailed in those years of her medical training, both by the evolution theory that was taught as fact in classes, and by the higher criticism that had crept into the church she attended. The Student Volunteer Movement meetings always had a reassuring, steadying effect on her, as did the letters she received from home. When she went to Boston for her internship after gaining her diploma in Toronto, she was outwardly unshakable.

'I'd give everything I own to believe as you do,' said the daughter of an Episcopalian Bishop, a divorcee, who was her senior in the maternity hospital there. The two of them had many talks about faith and about Christ, and when she made that remark Jessie kept silent. She did not want to disclose how often doubts and questions arose in her own heart. It was not until she got to Philadelphia, where she completed her internship, that she met someone to whom she could talk freely about the theological problems she was secretly trying to solve.

'Dr. Everett was a fine surgeon and a fine woman,' Jessie wrote many years later. 'I told her how shaky I felt and she talked with me at length and steadied me. Also the Bible classes she led helped me.' Then Jessie added a strangely revealing sentence. 'I never told mother any of these distressing doubts.' The child, sensitive to the reactions of loved parents, lived on in the increasingly proficient medical woman.

Her internship completed, she felt she was ready to go to China, but the Canadian Presbyterian Board had advised her not to apply until she was twenty-five. So she went with her mother to visit the ancestral home in Scotland, and once in the British Isles the whole course of her life was redirected. The objective remained the same, but the route by which she was to go to China changed.

While in Scotland she attended lectures at the Bible Training Institute in Glasgow and passed the exams. Then she went to London to take a course in tropical diseases and also to get a London degree. Once again she was among crowds of men, including many general practitioners who had come for post-graduate experience. Jessie crept into the classrooms as unobtrusively as possible and slid into a back seat, hoping she would not be seen. She dreaded the prospect of being pounced on by a lecturer during demonstrations, when a patient's symptoms were given and then diagnoses invited.

'I saw the backs of the doctors' heads when asked questions,' she related afterwards. 'If it was an English doctor I could see the back of his neck turn pink—but not the Americans!'

During her stay in London she lived at the headquarters of a missionary society—the China Inland Mission. The large, five-storied building at Newington Green had plenty of accommodation for missionary candidates and missionaries on furlough, and the young American doctor who hoped to go to China was welcomed. She found herself in a bedroom which happened to be next to the one occupied by the General Director and his wife, so it was usually the General Director's wife who knocked at Jessie's door at 6 a.m. each morning with a cup of tea for her. Jessie was overwhelmed, and even more so when she had read the newly published biography of the founder of the Mission, and realized that the gentle little person in her dressing-gown was actually the daughter of Hudson Taylor's sister Amelia. That biography moved her more than anything else she had ever read, and now here she was, at the very heart of things! The simple, earnest atmosphere of the place with its prayer meetings and its faith, its frugality and its happiness won her heart.

'God's leading was clear. Humbly I applied to the C.I.M., was accepted and sailed for China from London in 1913.'

*   *   *

She arrived at a crucial time in China's history. The Manchu dynasty had come to an end at last, the Republic had been born, and hopes for a new China were running high. As far as the C.I.M. was concerned, it was a well-established mission now, with centres reaching right across the country from the coast to the borders of Tibet, and with a membership of a thousand or more. The pioneering era was past, and although advances were always being made into the unevangelized areas and among remote tribes, the presence of Western missionaries was generally recognized and accepted by the authorities. It was an ideal time for the innovation of a woman doctor. Jessie McDonald was the first woman surgeon to join the mission, and a place was waiting for her.

A few miles south of the Yellow River, in the vast agricultural province of Honan, lay the city of Kaifeng, sprawling within its seven miles of city wall and spilling over in a haphazard fashion into the suburbs around. The sturdy northerners who inhabited it had not liked foreigners, and it was only after the disastrous Boxer uprising of 1900 that a C.I.M. missionary had managed to rent a couple of rooms in it. However, when he had been joined by another, who was a doctor, cautious interest had quickened into an eager demand for their services. Crowds gathered to listen to the preaching, and also see what the foreign doctor could do for their physical ills.

Because of this encouraging response a hospital had been built in one of the suburbs, but Dr. Whitfield Guinness, whose fame as a surgeon had spread far and wide, was still hampered by age-old tradition when it came to seeing women patients. The medical work desperately needed a woman doctor; there was not one in the whole great plain with its 35 million people. Could not this North American surgeon be designated to Kaifeng?

To Kaifeng she was sent. Her arrival was greeted with relief, for one of the doctors had just died from typhus, and Dr. Guinness was coping single-handed. His new colleague looked so young it was difficult to realize how well qualified she was, but she soon proved her worth, and as a person was 'nothing but a joy from the start,' Mrs. Guinness asserted.

Mabel Soltau thought so too. Mabel Soltau was a nurse from England who had recently joined the staff of the hospital, and as she and Jessie studied Chinese and worked together they struck up a friendship that was to last for life, and hold them together throughout their years in China.

The value of that relationship was inestimable, for not only in the work but in their social life each complemented the other. Jessie, for all her inner timidity, was a quick, vivacious sort of person, while Mabel who was quieter provided just the stable support she needed, both in the home they shared and the responsibilities they shouldered in the newly built women's hospital. Their united talents and skills were to open a door of opportunity for Chinese women whose lives might otherwise have been restricted to the home.

The revolution that saw the end of the Manchu dynasty was ushering in a new type of Chinese womanhood, emancipated from the foot-binding and mind-binding of the past. Now there were young women from wealthy homes who were actually eager to go to mission hospitals and learn the nursing and medical skills of the West. Their lives at home had ill equipped them for what would be required of them, it is true. The first probationer nurse to arrive was cultured and quite well educated, accustomed to slaves waiting on her, and when it was explained that the rising bell would sound at 6 a.m. she ejaculated, 'But I never get up till nine!' Nursing training held many problems for Miss Wen. Nevertheless, the day came when Jessie could claim that she was her left-hand man, just as Miss Soltau was her right. Graduation ceremonies at which the nurses received their diplomas were highlights of the year for the Canadian doctor and the English nurse who had watched over them through their training.

As the only woman doctor Jessie was naturally the one who had to deal with emergency calls from women, however difficult they might be. One surgical experience Jessie never forgot was that of operating on a young woman who had tried to commit suicide by swallowing some forty-odd needles. It was a tricky business, but Jessie succeeded in extracting them all, and the patient lived. Whether she was as grateful to the foreign woman doctor as were her parents is not recorded, but they were greatly relieved. The girl was shortly to be married, and it would have been a great loss of face if she had died in such a way just then.

There were opportunities of a different sort for the three Western doctors in the hospital in Kaifeng. They were in constant demand to lecture on health subjects to crowded audiences of townsfolk as well as students in college, and they were glad of the chance to do so. 'Ignorance of the laws of health necessitate something being done to open the eyes of the people to the dangers under which they are living,' wrote Dr. Guinness, who firmly believed that a fence at the top of a cliff was better than an ambulance at the bottom. With typhus, cholera, smallpox and tuberculosis wreaking havoc among the population, it was encouraging after a time to see food vendors in the streets covering their stalls with gauze to keep off the flies. 'Thus a beginning has been made.'

If things were going well in the C.I.M. hospital in Kaifeng, the same could not be said for the country as a whole. The Manchus had ruled with arrogance and cruelty, but at any rate they had ruled, which the new government seemed incapable of doing. Warlords arose, the country was divided, brigandage was rife and the roads were no longer safe for travellers. By the time Jessie left for her first furlough she had an uneasy feeling that the future might make more exacting demands than she had faced in the past, and she wanted to be as well prepared as possible for any situation that might arise.

It took some moral courage for a naturally retiring person like her to go to the County General Hospital in Los Angeles and ask for an interview with the superintendent. She was staying with relatives in California at the time, but knew no one who could give her an introduction, so although she confessed afterwards that she was scared stiff, she made the approach without one. She explained that she was a missionary doctor in China, needed an all-round medical brush-up, and would be very grateful if he would allow her the freedom to go to any department in his hospital to observe and gain experience.

The superintendent was somewhat taken aback. It was an unheard-of request.

'But I looked harmless, so he gave me a card,' Jessie reported afterwards with a characteristic chuckle. The staff at the hospital had a free and easy manner which surprised her, but they were very helpful, and when she asked where she could get as near as possible to the sort of conditions encountered during civil war, the answer was, 'Go to the down-town accident clinic in the worst part of town between 11 p.m. and 4 a.m.' So she went there, and got accustomed to emergencies involving people who had been injured in fights. 'And what about dealing with drunks?' The Salvation Army would help her there, she was told, so to the Salvation Army she went.

Not very long after she had returned to Kaifeng from her

112

furlough she and Mabel Soltau had their home invaded—peacefully, it is true, but it was more or less taken over for several weeks by Her Excellency, wife of the Governor of Honan. The Governor's little son was brought in at death's door, having already been unsuccessfully attended by scores of local doctors. He was placed in the sitting-room, where he could be constantly under the eye of the wonder-working doctor. There could be no suggestion of such an exalted little personage being put into a hospital ward, so there he remained in the sitting room for over a month, until he was well enough to go home. Various members of the Governor's household also took up their abode in the house, in order to help look after him. Medical missionary work was certainly providing an effective introduction into Honan's high society. 'We hardly knew ourselves when the great man's servants and family had all gone, the house felt so empty.'

The next incident of major importance to disturb the normal routine of hospital life was far more serious. There had been plenty of news and rumours of fighting between two powerful warlords, but one Saturday morning things came to a head. It was learned that no trains were running, that all communication with the outside world had been cut, and that the Governor and his family and entourage had beat a hasty retreat. Then train-loads of wounded soldiers began arriving, and the women's hospital suddenly changed its character as it filled up with wounded men, and the newly trained young women nurses were called into action.

'It was really amusing to see the men's faces as they came into the dressing-rooms and found Chinese girls telling them what to do, and attending to their wounds in the most matter-of-fact manner.' But they were in neither the position nor the mood to protest. Most of those brought in were from the defeated army and all they wanted now was to be eased of their suffering.

Dr. Walker and I were the only doctors. There was no time for operations at first. We got them classified, dressed and put to bed, then operated till late in the night, removing bullets, setting fractures, etc., and we have been at it ever since. They streamed in till we had nearly two hundred. The chapel floor was crowded. Several have died, more are dying—awful conditions, as you can imagine. Some of the faces haunt me. Their only hope is in us.

The upheaval lasted for some weeks, but eventually the triumphant General Feng entered the city to become the new Governor of Honan, and things settled down for a time. But peace did not last long. After another military coup the banditry and disorder became so bad, with anti-foreign feeling being stirred up, that the Mission authorities decided the hospital must be closed and the missionary staff withdrawn to Peking. Jessie went home for her second furlough.

Meanwhile, a new figure was emerging in China's politics—General Chiang Kai-shek. Under him the country was becoming more unified, and after two or three years it was decided that the hospital in Kaifeng should be reopened. But by this time Dr. Guinness had died. Jessie returned to shoulder heavier responsibilities than before, as the senior doctor there. It looked as though she would be working in more peaceful conditions, at any rate, with a stable government, and the opportunity to resume the training programmes that had already produced, over the years, a number of well-qualified Christian doctors and nurses, working now in various hospitals and centres.

But China, a naturally peace-loving nation, seemed destined to be plunged into war. While the Central Government was battling with the forces of Communism within China, her enterprising neighbour, the island kingdom of Japan, was growing stronger and stronger. Japanese gunboats in increasing numbers slid unobtrusively into Chinese waters, while her factories piled up munitions. The retreat of the Eighth Route army on its long march up to Yenan, in the mountains of the north, was barely over when the Japanese armies were pouring over China's borders, and she was mustering all her resources to stay their advance.

The confusion of those days was extreme. The trains running from the north and east came crowded with refugees fleeing from the invading army, with people clinging like limpets outside and on the carriage roofs. They surged along the city streets, laden with their belongings, seeking shelter in the overcrowded inns and courtyards, and especially in the churches and premises belonging to Roman Catholic and Protestant missions, which were considered safe from attack, since they belonged to the nationals of neutral countries. It was hard to resist the pleas of the hundreds who came begging for refuge. Running a hospital in such circumstances, especially when staff members became infected with the prevailing panic, was fraught with problems and emergencies. And all the time the rumours grew more alarming, and the sounds of gunfire drew nearer and nearer.

Aeroplanes circling overhead, the roar of cannons, soldiers running, armoured cars arriving, shooting in the streets... Kaifeng was taken. The Japanese were in control.

The city that had been so tumultuous became strangely silent, the streets deserted, as a pall of fear descended upon it, its inhabitants huddled trembling behind closed doors. Sturdy little alien warriors, armed to the teeth, disciplined but ruthless, manned the public buildings, guarded the gates and knocked peremptorily on doors to make their demands. Able-bodied men were conscripted to do heavy work, and officials who had been unable to escape were imprisoned if they refused to co-operate. The families who had not already sent their girls and young women off to relatives in the countryside tried to hide them now. Very few were successful in doing so...

The missionaries themselves were treated quite courteously at first. Their neutrality was respected, and medical work in the hospital continued more of less as before. However, after a time rumours reached them of a change of policy on the part of the invaders. Japanese soldiers were being billetted on some mission centres in remoter regions, restrictions were being imposed, and a generally more unfriendly attitude adopted towards American and British nationals. Then some demonstrations against them were organized, with reluctant Chinese forced to march around and shout slogans demanding that they leave.

With the Japanese authorities so obviously keen to see them depart, Jessie and her colleagues wondered what would happen to the hospital if they had to leave. Its closing would only add to the distress of the people of Kaifeng, but without a medical superintendent favoured by the authorities, how could it continue to function satisfactorily?

It was at this point that the international character of the Mission proved its value. If American and British nationals were frowned on by the invaders, those from Germany were smiled upon. A German doctor in charge would ensure that the hospital could be kept open, and that the gospel could continue to be proclaimed within its walls.

Such a doctor was found. He agreed to leave his own hospital and come and take over the one in Kaifeng from Dr. Jessie McDonald. With her colleagues she bid a reluctant goodbye to the people and the place she had loved and served for over twenty years and travelled to Peking. She hoped that when the war was over she might return to Kaifeng, but she never saw it again.

*   *   *

Directing missionary work in a country in the throes of civil war is fraught with difficulties. Directing missionary work in a country that is fighting back with all its military strength against a powerful invader is fraught with even greater difficulties. And when among displaced missionary personnel are a highly qualified doctor and nurse with

116

experience in running a hospital with a training programme for probationers, mission authorities can find themselves in a quandary.

The C.I.M. was in just such a quandary in 1940 regarding Dr. Jessie McDonald and her colleague Miss Mabel Soltau. To leave such a couple to kick their heels in Peking, doing sporadic 'field work' where they could, was too wasteful when there were vast areas in China completely devoid of the sort of medical help they were qualified to provide. The question was, where could they be sent without the likelihood of being uprooted again as the Japanese armies thrust further and further into the stricken country? Among the many matters that were discussed and prayed about in C.I.M. headquarters in Shanghai in those days was the possibility of opening a new hospital in the interior, sufficiently far from the main routes to be moderately safe, yet with a lifeline along which needed supplies could be brought.

There was just one province that seemed to provide the necessary requirements. The sunny, mountainous province of Yunnan, down in the south-west, was remote from the scene of war, yet it was now known as the back door into China. Over the famous Burma Road, that snaked its way across from Burma into Yunnan, convoy after convoy of trucks and jeeps were bringing in the only supplies that China could now import. The region through which the great highway passed was vulnerable to Japanese bombers, but unlikely to experience Japanese occupation. And in the plateau of Paoshan across which the highway passed, virtually no medical work was being done. In a town of 30,000 inhabitants, with an estimated 300,000 in the surrounding neighbourhood, the need for a hospital was obvious. The superintendent of the Mission's work in the province, John Kuhn, who with his wife Isobel lived among the Lisu tribespeople, was very keen on the idea. The outcome of all the discussions was that Dr. Jessie McDonald should be invited, with the help of Miss Mabel Soltau and

Dr. Frances Powell, a new worker, to go to Yunnan and open a hospital there.

On the face of it, it was asking a great deal of a woman in her early fifties, for it meant going to a strange and isolated place, and taking complete medical responsibility for a hospital where she would be several days' journey from other qualified surgeons to whom she could turn for consultation and help. Nor was that all. Before she could take responsibility for the hospital, she had to bring it into being. She must find suitable premises, choose equipment with a limited capital, recruit staff, all at a time when war was waging in Europe and Asia and communications were often delayed for months on end, or cut altogether.

Whatever may have been their initial reaction when the proposition was put to them, Jessie and Mabel ultimately accepted the suggestion, and set off from Peking in August to go to Yunnan. Their route took them via Shanghai, by ship down to Singapore, then up to Rangoon, in Burma.

They arrived there in January 1941, to find the place a sort of bottleneck in which missionaries trying to enter China by the back door found themselves jostled by military personnel and astute businessmen, all intent on the same objective. Not surprisingly, the missionaries found themselves at the end of the queue when it came to getting through Customs and finding the right officials.

'Either the government or the people here need to be wakened up a bit,' wrote Jessie rather irately after she had been there for several weeks. 'Such a place! Expensive, too. It's costing us exactly five times as much as in Shanghai.' Her impressions of Burma were vivid.

A place of golden pagodas, of brilliant patches of colour, sunset and flowers and birds and dress, brilliant yellows, greens, purples and reds and pinks. But we have little time for sightseeing. There seem just two tasks of importance here. Customs and transportation. Every second day is a holiday it seems. No one works much

... They are always having half days or weddings or auctions sales or 'Boats in'. Well, it is the effect probably of generations of easy living, a kind soil which produces an abundance without coaxing and makes a lazy people.

As she and fellow missionaries congregated there all applied their minds and their energies to getting several tons of luggage through Customs and then finding ways and means of getting it transported into China, her views on Burma and the Burmese became distinctly jaundiced. As for the British! They were censoring everything, as bad as the Japanese in north China.

However, in retrospect, she saw that things had gone quite well. The Customs official at Rangoon had taken pity on the woman who had been turned out of her hospital by the Japanese, and decided to let all her baggage through without charge. Then, after what seemed an interminable delay, she eventually broke the final ties with the Customs when, instead of searching everything she had, they allowed it all through without opening a single box. As she was responsible for some 138 of them it was just as well for her that the government (British) and the local officials (Burmese) were not looking for work unnecessarily. As she climbed into the front seat of the lorry on which she was to travel up to Lashio, near the China border, she felt for Fred Keeble, the C.I.M. treasurer, who was there to see her off. He was left in Rangoon with some five or six tons of supplies for missionaries and some of her own stuff, waiting to be transported into China. 'Look like being here for the duration,' he said, mopping his round rosy face and grinning ruefully. 'Keep on praying!'

She settled back in her seat, glad of the opportunity to relax and enjoy the beautiful scenery. She wrote from Lashio,

The first day the paddy fields, the second day jungle and hairpin bends over hills gradually rising. We passed

119

flowers of every colour, dense forest and jungle. Oh, it's good to be out of the heat! This town reminds me of a gold-rush town in America. Everyone busy and prosperous. Temporary buildings springing up overnight, made of bamboo and thatch roof. Motor trucks everywhere, from the most handsome new four-ton variety to the small local ones busy everywhere. American flags painted on some, usually accompanied by the Red Cross. The Bank of China trucks, the South Western trucks which truck for the Chinese Government.

She and her baggage, along with several other missionaries and their baggage, were accommodated in a classroom of a government school, and from there she set about trying to obtain transport across the border.

She scarcely knew where to begin, but prayer, faith and perseverance prevailed. Amid the hubbub of traffic, the coming and going of uniformed men, the mysterious errands of people on who-knows-what business, she finally discovered the Control Commissioner who was responsible for every truck going over the highway. She little realized as she entered his office how wide a door this man would open.

It could not be denied that right from the start Mr. Holmes was on her side. He really wanted to help her, but there was little he could do. He shook his head when she explained about those 138 pieces of baggage already in Lashio, and that there were some more left behind in Rangoon, and how she wanted to get them all across the border to Paoshan as cheaply as possible.

'Economical transport?' he sighed. 'There's a waiting list of several months long for that.'

Then she mentioned that she was planning to open a hospital.

Open a hospital! Mr. Holmes fastened on the piece of information like a dog on a juicy bone. She was going to open a hospital in China? Ah! This made all the difference. This was a special case. Hospitals were desperately needed.

He was acting on behalf of the Chinese Government and would have no hesitation in freeing some lorries to convey all the baggage she had mentioned into China as soon as it arrived from Rangoon. Let it all be brought at once!

Jessie started to explain that not everything in those five or six tons of goods in Rangoon was intended for the hospital. She felt she must be truthful about this. Quite a lot was just supplies for missionaries beleaguered by the war—soap and apple rings and castor oil, and some even bigger things, she admitted reluctantly. But Mr. Holmes stopped her. He didn't want to hear. There were some things he would prefer not to know. All he needed to know for practical purposes was that she was going to open a hospital. That was sufficient. Once everything was brought to Lashio trucks would be made available.

Everything! Jessie thought of the times in Rangoon when she and Fred Keeble and the others had been praying about that mountain of supplies which it seemed impossible to shift—and of the faith that can remove mountains. Through all the confusion and setbacks and delays God had been working to answer that prayer of faith.

She was exultant, but she kept her head. There was no point in wasting money on expensive communications, so the telegram she sent to Keeble in Rangoon was cryptic, merely telling him to come. 'Transportation and accommodation available.' She thought it would be sufficient.

She was right. It was all that Fred Keeble wanted to know.

'It is too long to tell you all about how quickly in the end we all got away,' Jessie wrote from Paoshan in China a fortnight later. 'The hold-up was so long, obviously the Lord was keeping us back, but when the time came the move went so smoothly and speedily that we could scarcely keep up with it.' The last of the missionary party from Rangoon arrived with the final consignment of goods on Saturday; on Sunday the truck owner came to tell them that if they could get everything loaded on his trucks on Monday they could be away on Tuesday. And so it came about, though not without some incidents involving three American servicemen who were quick with a gun, then a drunken Anglo-Burmese official who was eager for a fight, and the treasurer of the C.I.M., quickly deciding that valour in some cases is the better part of discretion, wading in to separate the contestants.

'What an entrance into China!' Jessie observed later when she was back again in the country. But it was a very different China from the one she had known in Honan. There it was flat and dusty: here it was hilly and fragrant. There the people were cheerful and ready to work: here they were morose and indolent, for Yunnan was one of the 'opium provinces' where it was cynically said that thirteen out of every twelve people took opium. She soon discovered that a major problem in running a hospital here would be to obtain servants to do the cleaning and the carrying. But in the early stages the difficulty was getting a hospital at all. The only available premises in Paoshan large enough to be converted into a hospital were the temples, and various suggestions and negotiations for obtaining one of them all fell through. Meanwhile, as Paoshan was a target for repeated attacks from Japanese bombers flying over from Indo-China, it was eventually decided to convert into a hospital the C.I.M. property in the neighbouring town of Tali, ten miles off the Burma highway, and higher up in the mountains.

There is a Pepys-like quality about Jessie's home letters during this period which give intimate and sometimes amusing glimpses into her life. She got the opportunity to go to Chungking in Szechwan province by plane, and travelled with the British Ambassador who wrapped himself in a rug and went to sleep with his mouth open. In Chungking itself she received a touching but very noisy welcome in church from someone who knew her in Kaifeng. 'Everywhere I run across Kaifeng people and they are homesick.' (The trek of one of the largest refugee movements the world has ever

122

known was in progress, as literally millions of Chinese fleeing from the Japanese invaders were pouring into the western provinces.) Chungking was riddled with caves and dug-outs into which people scuttled like rabbits when they heard enemy planes approaching.

In Chungking she also met Mr. Yin from Honan, who was now one of the financial heads of government and a very important official. Mrs. Yin, who had six children and as many servants, was delighted to see her, so that she could get away from housekeeping. Mr. Yin scolded her, she said, because the mosquito wiring was so dirty and the corners of the rooms were not swept. 'I should never have married,' she said with a laugh. 'I don't like looking after homes and kitchens. He is so tidy and orderly, and I am not.'

In Paoshan unexpected visitors sometimes arrived, one of them the British consul who was on a three-months' tour of his district.

He is red haired, wears a monocle, speaks with an Oxford accent and wears an Oxford tie. He travels on horseback, by preference, has a retinue of assistants, servants and twenty-odd house tents, etc. However, in spite of the fact that he has all the luxuries you could wish, he likes to come and have dinner with us. He called at the Kuhns's district in Lisu-land, and wherever there is a British missionary he looks them up—unnecessary, but he is a kind man.

They moved to Tali, which was smaller, cooler and as beautiful as a summer resort in Switzerland, with clear streams running over rocks, blue sky, fleecy clouds and a gem of a lake. Every prospect, in fact, was pleasing, and only man left anything to be desired. The carpenters and the masons, mooching around and smoking all day long, opium if they could get it, made her long for the workers of dear old Honan. 'But we must not say such—we are trying not to *think* such.' The best worker they had was their one-eyed probationer, who did the marketing, weighed the coal and

123

the lime and removed any stones, washed the clothes when the washerwoman failed to turn up and generally made herself useful.

She is an honest child with a sunny nature. I do want to get her a good glass eye. Oh, the things we need! And now money is frozen. You have money in the bank and you cannot get it out. You cannot get an American cheque cashed without permission from Washington. You cannot get English cheques cashed. No wonder the financial department of the C.I.M. in Shanghai is hard put to know what to do. Well, this is certainly not a suitable time to begin a hospital, and yet here we are. Our outpatients department will be ready in a few days' time.

They were hurrying now, sorting a miscellany of instruments obtained from a variety of sources, though acutely aware of their need of a sterilizer. They had a double incentive for seeing patients as soon as possible—to relieve suffering and to get some ready cash by selling medicine. Three of their trained assistants from Kaifeng joined them, and classes were started for the six probationer nurses who have enrolled.

In December 1941 the C.I.M. hospital in Tali was officially opened. In the same month Japan declared war on the U.S.A. and Great Britain by bombing, without any warning, American bases in Pearl Harbor, Manila and Hawaii.

Jessie heard about it the same day, for Pentecostal missionaries living in Tali had not only electric light but a radio as well, so they got all the news that way. 'Japanese forces land in Malaya ... Philippines invaded ... Penang raided ... Burma raided ... Hong Kong surrenders to the Japanese ...' It was World War II with a vengeance now. How would it all end?

*   *   *

It ended in Asia, after years of bitter fighting, on 14 August 1945, with the unconditional surrender of the Japanese following the dropping of the atomic bombs on Hiroshima and Nagasaki.

*   *   *

During that time the little hospital in Tali, built round three sides of a Chinese courtyard, had struggled to life and then put up a spirited fight for its own existence. It might be said to have been born prematurely, when a truck accident landed fourteen badly injured people at its doors before there were even any beds to lay them on. The equipment in Jessie's 138 pieces of baggage was pitifully little, and some other much-needed supplies were sent to the wrong places by mistake. The framework of the precious treadle sewing machine for instance, was welcomed with delight until the discovery was made that the machinery had gone to a city a thousand miles away. Some things were transported all the way up to Inner Mongolia, and over two years elapsed before they were eventually delivered in Tali.

There were problems with thieving servants, too, such as had rarely been encountered in Kaifeng. 'At the beginning our only trustworthy coolie was half blind, the water-carrier was paralysed in half his body, and the staff cook had epileptic fits every few days.' What was even more disappointing was the drop-out rate among student nurses who did not like hard work and whose educational standards were low. At the end of three and a half years only two had graduated, one of them the sunny-tempered young probationer for whom Jessie went to infinite pains to obtain a glass eye.

The marvel is that there were any graduations at all, for at one stage in the training scheme the hospital had been closed altogether. South-west China had suddenly become vulnerable with the Japanese invasion of Burma, and one night Paoshan was bombed so mercilessly that the city lay in ruins with 10,000 dead. 'If the Lord had answered our prayers in giving us our hospital building there, we'd have been among them,' Jessie and Mabel reminded each other. Then ensued the Burma Road panic, as news was received, richly embellished with rumours, that Japanese battalions were marching in. John Kuhn, acutely conscious of his responsibility as C.I.M. Superintendent, sent an urgent message to Jessie and her colleagues to get out as quickly as possible. Young Dr. Frances Powell had been ill for some time, so Mabel Soltau travelled out with her, and most of the Chinese staff dispersed.

'I did not know what I should do,' wrote Jessie later. 'Whether to leave or not. What of drugs and equipment?' To leave it all behind without any responsible person in charge at such a time would be asking for the looters to come in and help themselves. 'I was sure the Lord would keep us from making a foolish mistake, one way or the other.' She decided to stay, and was very thankful she was there when cholera broke out among the floods of refugees in the town. In two days she gave over a thousand inoculations, only stopping when the vaccine ran out.

'These are tough days, but the reward is great,' she wrote at that time. 'Tali has only one other doctor practising Western medicine and he is going. We are needed. It does not do to run away from duty—the only safe place is where God would put us.' And when eventually the crisis is over and things resumed their previous pattern, she admitted that she really enjoyed it all: '. . . you don't know the comfort it has been to be able to help these refugees, to give thousands of cholera injections or treatments.' Then she went on with a characteristic comment about hoping that her patience and digestion and love and sense of humour would hold out to the end.

She enjoyed her occasional trips to Chungking, China's wartime capital, too. She received V.I.P. treatment there. She stayed with Bishop and Mrs. Houghton, her friends Mr. and Mrs. Yin put their car at her disposal, and 'Uncle

Sam's' military planes always had a seat for that little woman doctor from down on the Burma border'.

So the years passed, with rumours and alarms, the ebb and flow of war, with shortages of money and supplies and an apparently endless series of last minute deliverances.

'I really get a thrill out of life,' she wrote once after a long spell of working single-handed.

You never know what the Lord will do next. Yesterday the only other white doctor between India and Kweichow came along offering me a holiday. And the things we needed and could not get! Some of those new *Sulfa* drugs. The one we need most is for pneumonia. We had almost none . . . But these last days various soldier boys have come in, sometimes with pockets full of bottles, things they looted (or salvaged) from Burma. We can often buy such drugs for a mere song. But the interesting thing is that the drugs they want to get rid of are the very ones we need.

She remembered the verse of Scripture that had been especially impressed on her mind when she set out on the long, roundabout journey from Peking to Yunnan. *'Your Father knoweth what things ye have need of before ye ask Him.'* She felt she could set her seal on its truth.

*   *   *

'Paoshan is a place where a clinic is badly needed. It's the business centre for the hill tribes of West Yunnan, has a population of some 370,000, yet the nearest hospital is in Tali, 250 kilometres and four mountain ranges away,' Jessie McDonald told a group in a medical conference in Shanghai, early in 1948. She was listened to respectfully, for her reputation as a pioneer doctor was well established. The

127

war against Japan was over, and although the Chinese Communists emerging from their base in the northern mountains were proving stronger than the scattered remnants of the Government's armies north of the Yangtze, a general conviction prevailed that they would never gain control of the whole country. Even the cautious pessimists who thought they might eventually do so, agreed that it would take them at least a decade. Meanwhile, there were unprecedented opportunities for evangelistic and medical work in the peaceful areas of the south and west, and those opportunities must be grasped. A group of well-to-do Chinese Christians had been stirred into action, and were prepared to finance clinics in remote regions if C.I.M. could provide the medical personnel. So it was that a couple of months later Jessie found herself living in a Ming-dynasty temple which the Paoshan city fathers had decided would be suitable for 'The Holy Light Rural Medical Service Paoshan Clinic affiliated with the China Inland Mission base hospital in Tali'.

The ponderous title was less confusing, though, than the work it all entailed for Jessie. As the senior doctor she had to remain for a long time in the clumsy set-up, camping out in a room with an earth floor and cracks in the wall through which she caught the indignant eye of a displaced idol. It worried her less than the fleas.

'This is truly the job for a younger person,' she wrote to her home folks late one night. 'If there were another doctor I'd go back to Tali for a time at least, but there are so many problems in the pot it would be selfish to run away.' She admitted that what she would like to do would be to 'fly to America and see you all and have a rest'. She little thought how that desire was to be fulfilled.

Things moved very quickly in 1948. The Chinese Communists made rapid advances, not only on the military front but through their agents working secretly behind the lines. The first intimation the missionaries in the Tali hospital had of the effectiveness of their propaganda was

128

when all the nurse probationers in one class went on strike. The dispute was no sooner settled than three of the nurses disappeared, leaving behind a note to say that they had gone to join the People's Army. A month later another left to join them. And the news over the radio was increasingly ominous.

On 10 December it was officially announced that the whole province of Yunnan had been 'liberated'. The Communists were in control. The information was imparted to the Yamen in Tali by telephone. The actual occupation took place on 25 December with almost the whole population of Tali turning out to welcome the soldiers as they marched in, right past the church where Christmas Day was being celebrated. As Jessie observed, it was a bit difficult to pay attention to the sermon.

The following day an official came and confiscated all the radio sets in the hospital. No more B.B.C. news! About a week later he came again, this time to interview each of the missionaries in turn. To their amazement he was accompanied by two of their runaway nurses, dressed now in official Communist uniform. A month or so after that four of the student nurses announced that they wanted to leave and offer their services to the People's hospital. They were quite polite, sorry to be causing any inconvenience, but they felt called to serve the people. That left only one student to graduate in a class that started with ten. It looked like the end of the nursing school.

Meanwhile, the normal pattern of life for the people of Tali was changing. Meetings were the order of the day: accusation meetings, political meetings, demonstrations, indoctrination classes, speeches over loud-speakers blaring out announcements and Communist policies and ideals. The pattern was the same all over China.

The hospital was careful to ensure that a representative group always went along to any public demonstration. It had received a black mark for not having sent one to welcome the army on Christmas Day, and dared not offend again. Useless to plead that a depleted staff would mean the patients suffered. The State came first, not the patient. More revolutionary still, from the traditional Chinese viewpoint, the State came before the family, before the parent. Jessie and her colleagues were dismayed to hear one day that a former probationer nurse, during a dispute over property, had publicly accused her mother of some wrong and as a punishment the mother had been made to kneel on cacti.

In spite of everything, however, the situation in Tali was fairly encouraging, and after eighteen months another class of probationer nurses was hopefully formed, while on Christmas Day the hospital compound was awakened by the sound of carol singing, and seven people were baptized. But things were very different elsewhere, as Jessie knew from private letters and reports received from time to time. Churches were being closed as Christians were accused of anti-Communist activities and thoughts, and especially of being spies for the agents of Western imperialism—the missionaries. Several missionaries were under house arrest, including Dr. Rupert Clarke on the Tibetan border who like herself, was responsible for a Holy Light Rural Medical Clinic.

It was not really a great surprise when early in January 1951, the solemn news came from C.I.M. headquarters in Shanghai that after much prayer and painful thought it had been decided that the whole Mission should be withdrawn from China.

So the end of her missionary career was in view, and five months later it ended. The long negotiations for the taking over of the Tali hospital by the Communist government were completed, and in June she left Tali for the last time.

'We might have asked if it was all worth it,' she said later, 'had it not been for the last three months in Tali.' That had been the crowning period of her ten years in Yunnan, as she had seen and heard the fearless testimony of the Christians of the staff in the hospital. Knowing that they would now have to work for an atheistic regime they had mobilized their resources, were openly attending church services, and early every morning met to pray together. 'That meeting means so much to us, we are determined it shall continue, even if it means getting up an hour or two earlier to fit it in,' they told her. She never heard from them again, and she did not want to bring them under suspicion with the Communist authorities by trying to keep in touch with them. But years later she heard 'by the grapevine' that there were two beacon lights burning in Yunnan. They were in Tali and Paoshan.

Dr. Jessie McDonald returned to North America in 1952, where she made her home with her brother and sister in law in California. Here she became naturalized as a citizen of the U.S.A., and died on 6 January 1980.

God has been speaking to me recently about the love needed to do His work. Love for Him and others must be the supreme motive. Love must be the source from which all my actions spring. Love for the Lisu, in spite of fretting irritations, as they throng my shack. Love for the Thai when I am disturbed by those who want a needless injection. Love for my fellow workers when resentment would creep in or self-love blot out their need. So as I labour I remember my past mistakes and God helps me to be patient and kind.

How changed is one's outlook when love is the motive for all one's actions, all one's missionary labours. My hasty impatient word is quelled, I learn to put myself in the patient's place, or in the place of a visitor, or a tired fellow worker. Climbing a mountain is for love of Him, lack of privacy, lack of comforts, lack of fellowship, loneliness and all that is involved in working among a mountain tribe when done for love of Him becomes a precious opportunity to show how much we love Him.

Extract from one of the last letters Lilian Hamer wrote to her friends.

6. Uphill All the Way

Lilian Hamer

Whether Lilian Hamer was actually turned out of her home, or whether she ran away from it is not quite clear. What is certain is that one Monday morning in 1937, at the age of twenty-five, she emerged from it in tears, leaving an infuriated father behind. She had been on tenterhooks the whole weekend, trying in vain to pluck up courage to tell him she had given up her job as a shop assistant because she had been accepted for nursing training in the local hospital (now Bolton and District General Hospital). Like all the rest of the family, she feared his temper and she knew he would not approve of what she was doing, especially as she wanted to become a nurse in order to do missionary work in China. As she expected, he got into a rage when eventually he was informed, and ordered her out of the house. 'I picked up my case and ran,' she told her friends afterwards. Life for her had always been overshadowed by her irascible parent, but all the same the complete break from home saddened her. She kept in touch with her mother and sister, but knew she was no longer a member of the household. So started her nursing training.

Five years had passed since the day when she stood up at the close of an evangelistic meeting to signify her faith in Jesus Christ and determination to be His disciple. From that time a new sense of purpose had inspired her. She was a mill worker, as she had been from the age of fourteen when she left school, but now she was convinced that God had a different plan for her. She did not know what it was, but she took the obvious steps of attending church regularly, studying the Bible and teaching in Sunday School. She set about improving her meagre education at evening classes, too, in practical as well as academic skills, including elocution and first aid.

Then she attended a meeting in Bolton organized by the China Inland Mission. She was deeply stirred, and read some of the Mission's books. The way ahead began to clear. God wanted her in China with the C.I.M. She was sure about that.

It was as well that she could not foresee what a long and uphill climb lay before her. Her first tentative enquiries about joining the mission elicited little encouragement. Chinese was an unusually difficult language for those unaccustomed to study. She was already twenty-five and had no special training. It was suggested that if she were a qualified nurse she might stand a better chance of being accepted, and so she worked for three years to gain her S.R.N. She applied again, and was advised to add midwifery to her qualification. Then she went to Redcliffe Missionary Training College for two years, where a full programme of intensive Bible study and practical experience in teaching and preaching made new demands, but added another qualification. She had done all that she could do. It was 1943 now, and she was over thirty, but as sure as ever that she should go to China. She made a formal application to the C.I.M. during her last term at college, filled in the necessary forms, and travelled to London to meet the members of the Ladies' Council. If they approved of her, they would pass on their recommendation to the London Council, the body with the authority to accept or refuse her.

To her it was the most important day of her life. For the first time after nearly nine years of waiting she was to be officially interviewed by the Mission with which she passionately longed to go to China. World War II was at its height, and air raids over London were daily occurrences, but to Lilian they were far less awe-inspiring than the

Ladies' Council. Some of its members were quite elegant; one or two, like Miss Mildred Cable, were famous, and all seemed very confident. Lilian, conscious of her mop of curly hair and marked Lancashire accent, felt very insignificant among them. They looked at her kindly but appraisingly, and asked her some questions. Rather irrelevant some of those questions seemed. She was very surprised when Miss Mildred Cable, intrepid pioneer in the Gobi desert, asked,

'Can you play the piano?' Playing the piano seemed to have nothing whatever to do with missionary work in China, but she knew she must answer, and felt it would go against her if she did so in the negative.

'Yes,' she said firmly. Then, after a momentary pause, she added, 'With one finger.' This raised a laugh, though as Lilian said later, it was no laughing matter to her. The interview over, she returned to College to await the verdict.

When it came it shattered her. However gently the blow was delivered, however softly cushioned with encouragement regarding God's will for her life, the stark fact faced her that her offer of service had not been accepted. The C.I.M. had turned her down.

The Principal of the College, who had given a good report of her and was nearly as surprised as Lilian herself, was dismayed at the depth of the girl's disappointment. 'She's breaking her heart,' she told her colleague anxiously, and to Lilian it seemed that that was what was happening. The very mainspring of life had been snapped, the motive that had urged her on through all those years of training was gone. Had she been younger she might have waited and applied again later, but very few people were accepted if over thirty, and she was already thirty-one. This was the end of her hopes, and she crumpled under the blow.

It has to come to this sometimes, when something is out of alignment. Unless the foundation is right the building will be unsafe, however strong it may appear. Lilian had been brought to this crisis, not to stop her but to steady her.

When the storm of grief had spent itself, and she was quiet, though despairing, it was as though a still small Voice spoke.

'Which comes first—Me or China?'

So this was it. Without realizing it, she had put China first. It had become almost an obsession, and it was not easy to relinquish it, but she knew she must.

'Do you love me more than these?' the risen Lord had asked Peter. Now the same question was confronting her. 'Do you love Me more than China?' She bowed her head, facing the implications in that question. It might involve giving up all hope of ever going to China, and instead settling down in her own country to a humdrum nursing career. How strong and how deep had been the conviction that she should go to China she had not realized until now. It had coloured her life for years. Now the question 'Which comes first—Me or China?' had to be answered.

'Lord, you are first,' she whispered at last. 'I'll serve you anywhere, even if it is to be in England. It doesn't matter where.'

So simple yet so basic was that act of submission. To China with Christ, in the C.I.M. had been the fixed order of things in her mind. Now it was with Christ—anywhere. And within a fortnight it became clear that it was to be with Him to China, after all. She learned that the British Red Cross was preparing to send a medical unit to that country, and was open to receive applications from people with suitable qualifications and references. She applied and was accepted. Several months were to elapse before the Unit could depart for China, however, and she had no regular income.

'But where is the money coming from?' a friend asked in surprise when Lilian told her that she hoped to take a course in Chinese at the School of Oriental Languages while she was waiting to go. God would send it if it was what she ought to do, Lilian replied. She had learned that God had various ways of providing what she needed, and in this case it was the British Red Cross that paid. 'They must think

136

very highly of her!' the Principal of Redcliffe noted with satisfaction. A little basement room had been fitted out for Lilian in the college so that she could live in London as cheaply as possible, and it was noticed that she always left very early each day, so that she could use the language records before the other students arrived. The progress she made was so good that when the Red Cross medical Unit, consisting of two doctors and herself, eventually set off for China, she was put in charge of it.

The journey overland to Calcutta, then by air over the Himalayan foothills, brought them into China in the spring of 1944. They were sent to a city where a human flood of refugees crowded the streets, while wave after wave of wounded soldiers were brought in from the front and laid wherever there was available accommodation. Some were in such a condition that immediate action was called for. On one occasion Lilian, a mere nurse, performed an amputation by the side of the road.

It was a bewildering situation for the little Red Cross Unit. They were in a strange land, billetted on people, some European, some Chinese, who were more aware than they of what was going on, and who were increasingly alarmed by news from the fighting line. Almost before they knew what was happening the Unit was whisked away, leaving most of its equipment behind, and within two months of arriving in China it had been disbanded. Lilian, still under the direction of the British Red Cross Commissioner in China, received a new posting. She was transferred to a Canadian hospital in the western province of Szechwan, in which lay the city of Chungking, wartime capital of China.

It was here that the emergency headquarters of the China Inland Mission had been established, after the Japanese attack on Pearl Harbor which brought the U.S.A. and Great Britain into the war against Japan. And it was here, one year after arriving in China, that the great desire of Lilian's heart was fulfilled. 'For nine years I have been training and waiting for the way to open for me to come out to China in the fellowship of the China Inland Mission,' she had written to the Director there, explaining her position. 'If there is any possible hope of my joining the Mission now or in the future, could you let me know?' The culmination of several months of uncertain correspondence, with delays and loss of letters due to wartime conditions, came on 4 April 1945 when she kept an appointment to meet the China Council of the C.I.M. in Chungking. When she emerged from the compound later that day and descended the narrow, winding streets of the city to get on the jeep that would take her to the airfield to her next assignment, she did so as an accepted candidate of the Mission. As soon as she had fulfilled her contract with the Red Cross she would become one of the fellowship and start her life as a fully accredited member of the C.I.M.

A year later she was working in the hospital in Tali, near the Burma border, recently opened by Dr. Jessie McDonald and Miss Mabel Soltau.

*   *   *

'Who are they? Where do they come from?' Lilian asked as she watched two girls walk across the hospital compound, their brightly coloured skirts swinging, silver ornaments jangling. They were not Chinese, she saw that at once. Quite apart from their dress, the easy way in which they moved about and a certain diffidence in their demeanour distinguished them from the people of Han. The tribal people from the mountains were somewhat ill at ease among the plain dwellers when they came down to the crowded markets and were usually eager to get back to their wild, free hillsides. 'Are they Tibetan?' She had seen a number of Tibetans, bold-eyed and very picturesque on their sturdy ponies, when they had come down for their annual fair near the city, and they had captured her imagination. These two girls were dressed rather like them, and she was interested.

No, she was told. There was a certain similarity in dress,

138

but these girls were not Tibetan. They were of the Lisu tribe, and lived far away to the west, in the canyons of the two great rivers, the Mekong and the Salween. J. O. Fraser had pioneered among them, as she knew, and there were now many little Christian communities up there in the mountains. John and Isobel Kuhn and others were working among them, and always singing the praises of their beloved Lisu. They had hoped at one time that the mission hospital might have been opened nearer to them, rather than here in Tali, but it was decided that the population was too scattered and the area too remote for the only mission hospital in west Yunnan. The Kuhns had sighed regretfully, but agreed that the greater number of people had the prior claim. The Lisu would have to wait.

At one time during those first few post-war years it seemed possible that Lilian might be appointed to provide a medical service to the tribal people in the mountains. This is what she wanted. Her sympathy had been aroused as she saw the condition of some of those who had made their way down to the streets of Tali, dishevelled, dirty and sick, the victims of opium. But she was needed in the hospital, especially when the matron returned home on furlough and she was appointed to take her place. Once again, the Lisu would have to wait.

Lilian got on extremely well with Chinese and tribespeople alike. Perhaps they sensed in her one for whom life had always been an uphill struggle in practical matters. Poverty and friction in the home in her early years had equipped her to understand instinctively the difficulties of daily living most of these people had to contend with. Conditions in the small terraced house in which she grew up, in a north of England mill town, had not been so very different from those in the courtyards of Tali.

'Her patients loved her,' Dr. McDonald wrote of her, 'as did also the student nurses. She did not mind how long her hours, how often she was called, or how little sleep she had ... When we found she was quite anaemic we tried to cut down on her work, but she would have none of it. Her influence was always for good.' Then Dr. McDonald added a penetrating comment on Lilian's ability by defining it as 'expendability, indefatigability, imperturbability, stick-at-ability, availability and with it all, amiability'.

If the expectations of peace and stability in China after the long war years had materialized, it is probable that Lilian would eventually have been released from hospital duties to go and work among the tribes. As it was, the civil war that had been held more or less in abeyance during the Japanese invasion flared up with renewed vigour after V.J. Day in August, 1945. The Communists gained ground rapidly, not only on the battlefronts but by effective infiltration. By 1948 meetings propounding their doctrines were being held all over Yunnan, and soon local units were rising up to seize power. Tali fell to them without a shot being fired. Before the close of 1948 General Mao Tse-Tung had proclaimed the People's Republic of China, Generallissimo Chiang Kai-shek and his Nationalist Government had retreated to the island of Taiwan, and the civil war was literally 'all over bar shouting'.

It was the beginning of the end as far as Christian missionary work was concerned. The various missions withdrew one by one, the C.I.M. being almost the last to do so. From all over the country, however, reports were being received of the added difficulties church members were experiencing due to the presence of Western missionaries. The pressure from church members themselves on the Mission to withdraw was the deciding factor for the C.I.M. leaders in their solemn consultations at headquarters in Shanghai. The time had come. The Mission must move out of China.

Early in 1951 the edict was received in Tali that the hospital must be handed over to local Chinese authorities and all the missionaries apply for exit visas to leave the country. It took several months to accomplish. Even after the negotiations with the Communist authorities had been completed there was a long delay before exit visas were issued, and it was not until May that Lilian set foot in the British Crown Colony of Hong Kong. By that time the next step had been made plain for her. The closing of China was not to mean the end of the Mission, as she had at first feared, but merely a change of location. Now the plan was to move into other countries of the Far East, including the legendary little kingdom of Thailand.

The northern boundaries of Thailand merged into the great mass of mountains that rolled, range upon range, up to the China border, and over those mountains were scattered the same tribes she had seen in Yunnan. They were accessible no longer through China, but it was as though a back door were quietly opening whereby they could be reached from a different direction. A couple of the men missionaries who already had experience in tribal work had been there to assess the situation, and it had been decided that John and Isobel Kuhn should head up a team to settle in north Thailand. Lilian was one who volunteered to join them, and after a furlough in England she arrived in Bangkok in July, 1952, eager to press on and up to the mountains of the north.

The group of displaced missionaries there were acutely conscious of the disadvantage of being among people whose language they did not understand. This applied especially to the older ones. Allyn Cooke, for instance, at over sixty years of age, might have decided that a short crash course in Thai was beyond him, and that it was time for him to retire. However, this is not the way he thought. For nearly forty years he had lived among tribal people in China, preaching to them, praying for them, loving them, and while God still gave him strength to walk and even climb he would continue to seek them. He would learn as much Thai as was necessary to make himself understood, then he would hire carriers to lead him up to the hills where the tribes lived. He might meet some among them who could speak Chinese.

His faith and his tenacity were rewarded. He met Old Six

on the Maesalong Ridge. Old Six, a jovial, middle-aged member of the Yao tribe, was the headman of his village, and he spoke Chinese. It was an eight-hour journey, mostly on foot, to get to his home, and when Allyn Cooke arrived there for the sixteenth time to reason with him of sin and righteousness and judgment, Old Six amazed him by announcing,

'This Jesus you've been talking about has saved me from my sin.' Allyn Cooke barely had time to take this in when Old Six continued,

'You also said He has a Holy Spirit. Well, this Holy Spirit has told me it is wrong to smoke opium.' Allyn Cooke nodded dumbly, listening as in a dream 'So now I am going to Chiengrai, to the Christian doctor there. He will help me to break it off. I'll travel back with you.' On that memorable journey the Holy Spirit told Old Six something else. The life-strings fastened around his wrists, tied there at his birth as a talisman against disaster, were quite useless.

'I don't need these,' said Old Six, looking at them reflectively. 'I'm a Christian now,' and off they came. Old Six remained in the Presbyterian Hospital for ten days and returned to the Maesalong Ridge free of the craving that had dogged him for twenty-six years of his life, and quite settled in his mind that everything he had heard about Jesus Christ was true and that he, Old Six, now belonged to Him.

It was the most significant event in the early progress of the gospel among the tribes of north Thailand, though he had to put up with a considerable amount of opposition from his fellow tribesmen as the result of his flagrant desertion of the spirits. Who knew what vengeance they would now wreak on the Yao of Maesalong Ridge? He had broken off his life-strings, he refused to sacrifice to the demons, he had departed from the way of the ancestors to follow another religion—not the religion of the dreaded and detested Thai, it is true, but the religion of the white man from beyond the seas, which was nearly as bad. When the missionaries from the plain came to visit, which, aware of

142

the issues at stake, they did frequently, the villagers viewed them with mingled surprise, suspicion and resentment. However, there are limits beyond which it is not wise to go in ignoring a headman, and Old Six insisted that they be received. If he invited these white foreigners to come and preach no one could stop them, not even his wife, though she could make things very unpleasant for them if she was out of humour. However, since one or two of the white women who came were able to treat various ills and wounds in a surprisingly effective manner, public opinion began to veer in their favour.

Lilian was one of those white women. With a bamboo staff and a shoulder bag, accompanied by one of the younger missionaries, she would trudge over the muddy rice fields, up the slippery trail to the village on the Ridge, and stay for several days at a time in Old Six's home, dispensing simple medical remedies, binding up wounds and ulcers, showing Bible pictures and trying to explain them with the few Yao words she had learned.

During those visits she saw the inner life of these people on the sunlit mountainsides. For all their colourful costumes and ready smiles, they were dogged by fear. Fear of crop failures, fear of Thai officials, fear of Communist infiltrators and above all, fear of the demons who lurked in the trees, the streams and the rocks, revealing their malignity openly through wind and storm, secretly through disease and disaster.

Added to their fears was the curse of opium. It was at once the livelihood of the people and their destruction. Along the narrow, ill-defined trails that spread like a web over the vast, forest-clad mountains of south-east Asia travelled the opium runners, plying their illegal but lucrative trade. In the hidden folds of the hills, fields of poppies proved to be the crops that brought in the most money. In obscure areas in the market towns bargains were struck that were satisfactory to both sides. But in little huts in tribal villages men's lives and energies were trapped and dissipated as they lay smoking 'the happy pipe'.

It was mainly the plight of these drug addicts, and the desire of some of them for deliverance from the craving, that prompted the Yao to build a little hut for Lilian on the Ridge, and urge her to come and live among them, providing her with the opening she had so earnestly prayed for. Eric Cox, of long experience among the tribes in China, with his wife Helen, had moved into a little house on the Ridge, and with them so close at hand the Mission leaders agreed it would be safe for Lilian, a single worker to live there. So commenced her life among the Yao. It proved to be only a step towards the fulfilment of her desire to reach the Lisu.

'My house is set on a hill and can be seen by all around,' she wrote. 'It is a one-roomed shack with split bamboo walls and a mud floor. It is open to all the curious, but I have tried to divide my room into two by a rug and some pieces of plastic. I have no private life whatever.'

She continued later,

Tonight, as I sit in my shack writing to you, shadows all around except for the light on my table, I hear someone coming up the hill in my direction. He is afraid because of the demons and the darkness, so as he climbs he chants to them. His voice, a monotonous drone, draws near and passes on to visit my heathen neighbour. Darkness all around me, demon power enslaving the people until they are ruled by fear. Yet as this lamp on my table by its light dispels the shadows, so God has given to me this glorious light of the gospel to shine out to all around.

She always saw things like this, in the context of spiritual rather than natural forces. The battle to deliver the drug addicts from their craving was a battle against Satan, to be waged by prayer and by constantly proclaiming the power of Jesus Christ the Lord to save those who trusted in Him,

144

as much as by the regularity with which medicine and vitamin tablets were handed out, or activities supervised.

'The course is completed and all have come through triumphantly, having known the power of your prayers and ours,' she wrote some months later, reporting on the twelve opium addicts she had been treating. 'But the evil one has not finished with them, and he is attacking them in subtle ways. We could not expect the devil to accept the deliverance of these twelve without a struggle. The fight is on and each one needs the covering of your prayers.'

She knew that there was little hope of a lasting deliverance from the opium craving unless the medical cure was accompanied by spiritual healing. Without the strengthened will and inspiration of hope that only Christ could give, the former addicts would only be back where they were when they first started taking the narcotic. When demon shelves remained in the home and unbelief in the heart, the lure of the short-lived false peace of the pipe usually proved too strong. Although she had stipulated that she would only give the course of treatment to those who were believers, there were inevitably some who made a false profession, and she had several disappointments as one and another of those who had known deliverance lapsed into the old habit. Nevertheless, it was evident to all that they had been healed, and if they went back to the old habit it was their own fault.

The news got around on the hills and into the tribal villages that there was a white woman living on the Ridge who had medicine that could heal opium addicts. The only disadvantage in the treatment she gave was that she continually preached about one Jesus, who she asserted was stronger than the demons, and in whom they must trust if they really wanted to be delivered permanently from the opium craving.

This would have proved too strong a deterrent to the Lisu in the village of Tsaba had it not been for Li Chou the silversmith. Li Chou was a Chinese, and had been successfuly cured of the opium craving by Lilian's methods, becoming a believer in Jesus into the bargain. The change in him was so evident when he returned to Tsaba that the headman was impressed. Perhaps this white woman could be persuaded to come and live in Tsaba and heal people's sicknesses and cure them of the opium habit? They built a little hut on stilts, sent an urgent invitation to Lilian to come and preach to them, and on her arrival led her to it and said proudly, 'This is yours!' The shack was not too strongly built, as became evident that evening when a crowd gathered in it to listen to the gramophone on which Lilian played gospel records in Lisu. They all suddenly fell tumbling in a heap three feet below on the ground. The floor had given way. Not that it mattered much. 'Don't worry, we can soon mend it!' she was assured when laughter had subsided. The floor was hoisted up and tied more firmly, and she lived on it for several days for, as she wrote,

'I have brought no furniture with me, so I sit, eat and sleep on the floor. The roof is so low I am continually in a stooping position. Backache and tiredness, together with a little dismay are what I feel at the moment. Dismay at the stupendous task committed to my single-handed care. However, I do not mind if only the Lisu will turn to the Lord.

She had come to another turning-point in her life. On 18 April, exactly ten years after she arrived in China, she made up her mind to move up to Tsaba for good. The Lisu there had promised to build her a larger house if she would do so, and no arguments on the part of the fellow missionaries against the scheme would move her from her decision. 'The Yao in Maesalong have Eric and Helen Cox, but the Lisu in Tsaba have no one,' was her irrefutable argument. Useless to point out that they were two while she was only one, and a women at that. The Lord would be with her, she countered, and won her point. Even when she arrived in Tsaba a couple of weeks later and found that the promised house had no

146

roof, and part of the foundation had been washed away, she elected to remain. The missionary who had escorted her pleaded in vain that she should return with him to the plains and wait until the house was really ready for her. She had come to Tsaba, and in Tsaba she would remain.

It was there that Isobel Kuhn, touring with her husband the areas where the north Thailand team were settling among the tribes, came on her one day in 1954.

With two Christian carriers to carry our bedding and some tinned food we had brought for Lilian, we started up the hill. Up, up through the silent trees and woods we climbed gently, and after about two hours John called out, 'There it is!' Sure enough, to our right the brow of the opposite hill fell away in the familiar slope of cleared ground, with bamboo houses clustered at the top and also scattered over the slope. My heart beat fast as we turned off on to the trail that led to the village. There, somewhere, was an English girl, living all alone ... We gave the Australian bush-call which we have always used in the mountains, and soon a short, curly-haired figure with a very fair skin appeared in the doorway of the new long little shanty at the end of the trail and waited there beaming at us.

The Kuhns stayed in Tsaba for the weekend, John preached several times in his excellent Lisu, but Isobel reported with her usual honesty later,

The results of our visit, humanly speaking, were not much. The two men who had talked before about burning their demon altars if a white pastor came to help, took panic, and one of them turned back. The other said he would burn his altar after he had 'escorted his ancestors' in the seventh month ... We were able to help Lilian with the Lisu language and with some suggestions for teaching children, but that was all. So we came away,

147

leaving Lilian alone at her front line outpost. John was determined to secure a fellow worker for her as soon as possible.

A fellow worker for Lilian Hamer. This was seen by all concerned as the most urgent need. The strain of living alone, among a people whose language she barely understood, in very primitive conditions, was considered to be too great, especially when there was political unrest in the countryside. Lilian herself was conscious of it, as her letters sometimes revealed. On one occasion, when contending factors in Tsaba quarrelled over the site of a house that was being built for her and she had to watch it being pulled down, she wrote words which revealed the conflict going on in her own mind.

As I write I can hear the men pulling down the house. The new site is not so good and certainly will not be peaceful. It would seem as if the spirits in the lofty house on the hill are laughing triumphantly as they watch. But the missionary at the foot of demon hill stands at the door of her shack and laughs too, for a great victory shall be the end of this seeming failure,

she continued defiantly, her confidence strong as she wrote. Yet in the same letter she admitted,

How I would love to escape from it all. I find it very hard to endure. Things were going so well; the children were learning to read and to write so quickly. I am hoping to have a fellow worker some day. For twelve months I have been alone, since there has been no one to send for my help. However, whether alone or with a companion, the Lord is able to work. Sometimes the fewer the workers the greater the work He can do.

Very few could have endured the gathering sense of evil

148

around that tiny bamboo hut surrounded by demon-worshipping tribespeople, listening far into the night to the monotonous, rhythmical stamping of feet and the beat of weird music, and encountering disappointment after humiliating disappointment, alone. But the cheerful, sturdy Lancashire lass, who had doggedly gone on in the face of constant discouragements at home, always rose above the sense of desolation that threatened to submerge her in the more rugged conditions of her life now.

At the end of the day her little shack was emptied of the Lisu visitors who came for medicine, to learn, to talk, to listen to 'the music box that speaks our language', leaving her drained and weary; but her loneliness then had a special result; the enrichment of her mind through reading. She loved books. When friends enquired what they could send to her, she asked for books, giving a list of the classics that she specially wanted.

She could become completely absorbed in a well-written story, returning from it to her workaday world as though she had been for a brief but stimulating holiday. And in books on the spiritual life she found a satisfaction of soul that only those who know long solitude can enjoy. Coming across words and phrases that perfectly expressed her own inarticulate thoughts and aspirations she rejoiced as though she had suddenly and unexpectedly met an intimate friend. Here was another spirit who had felt exactly as she, with whom she knew, in a mystical sense, a fellowship that transcended time and distance. Sometimes what she read opened up new vistas, as expressed in four simple lines which impressed her in her reading,

> Upward compelled by strong desire,
> On to the summits high and higher
> Glows holy purpose like a fire,
> Forward and Godward we aspire.

She had an effective way of passing on the inspiration she

herself received through her reading. Her formal education had been brief and somewhat meagre, but by her own choice and efforts her mind as well as her vocabulary had been enriched, and in her little shanty on the hillside letters were written which reached an ever widening circle of readers. They contained such a wealth of vivid description combined with spiritual insight that a letter from Lilian Hamer was eagerly welcomed and passed on for others to read.

The writing of those letters was to Lilian herself the outlet she needed for self-expression. Without a companion to share her thoughts, the readers of her letters became the ones with whom she communicated. She was already well known through what she had written, and when she returned home on furlough in 1955 she received so many requests to speak at meetings it was difficult to fit them all in. When it became evident that her gift with words by her pen was equalled by her gift with words as a speaker, she was in greater demand than ever. With her lively descriptions of her life among the Lisu her experiences were recounted before spellbound audiences: the long, hard journeys over muddy rice fields; her consciousness of battle; the animosity of the witch doctors; the entrance to a village blocked by a bamboo screen smeared with the blood of an animal that had been sacrificed. 'The village was closed to us. As we stood there in the rain, the awful struggle in which we are engaged and the reality of demon power came over us. That closed door, that blood-smeared screen, and the Lisu village whose people are afraid of us present a challenge to me that the blood of Christ shall be the only sacrifice they acknowledge.'

The lawlessness of the remote hillsides: the murderer who had returned from his hiding place in the mountains, and calmly came to her little clinic for treatment; the sharp, sudden sound of gunfire a few days later, when she wondered if the Communists had come over the border, and the shock of horror when she learned that retribution had followed the murderer, as the avengers of blood had captured him, then further taken the law into their own hands by beheading him.

'Such is the lawlessness and sin existing in a heathen village. It is darkness that can be felt—murder, hatred, greed, drunkenness, a people without hope and without God.'

Nor had that been the end of the episode. Fear of what would happen when the Thai authorities got wind of the affair had gripped the villagers, and early on Sunday, when she was hoping some would come to the evening service, she had realized that the whole village was on the move.

I saw whole Lisu families fleeing, the little children clinging to their mothers' skirts, older folk carrying iron cooking pots, blankets, oil lamps. I stood outside my door and watched this wholesale evacuation of the people I had served and loved, mourned and wept over. They could not say they had never heard, but my heart was sad. It seemed again as though the last twelve months was wasted labour.

But that had not been the end, either. 'Already we see the first streaks of dawn! All was not lost. My dear old Lisu grannie could not pass me by. She did not want to leave, but was forced to by her family. She brought me a parting gift of eggs and said, "I will not forget to pray to Jesus every day!" She did not know much, but her faith was real.' And later that day Lilian held a Sunday service after all, for the Chinese silversmith and one of the Lisu headmen had decided to stay. 'So I started all over again with the families who were left, and the new Lisu families who began to move in to occupy the empty houses.'

This missionary certainly had a story to tell. More than that, she had a message to deliver. Her personal dedication was a stinging challenge to the lethargic and complacent, an encouragement and an inspiration to the committed. When requests came from the Mission headquarters in South

Africa for a missionary speaker to visit various cities in the Union, Lilian was the one who was asked to go. It meant delaying her return to Thailand for some months, but it was worth it, for some young people there heard God's call to service through her.

It was with a strange sense of foreboding that she returned to Thailand at the end of 1956. The months that lay behind her had been full of variety, travel and human companionship made easy by the common language and her familiarity with the ways of the Western world. Now it was back to the isolation of the lonely hills among a people whose tongue she understood only imperfectly, whose customs were different. When she arrived it was to find that she could not even return to the place and the people she had known before, for the Lisu in the village of Tsaba had all moved away, and no one knew where they were.

However, there was one factor in the situation which transformed it for her. At last she was to have a fellow worker. Dorothy Collingwood had been designated to work among the Lisu, and would join her as soon as she had completed the necessary Thai language study.

By the time she had done so Lilian had located some of the Lisu from Tsaba. They had moved to a mountain range that could be reached from the rather remote market town of Prao, lying in the plain between two highways, and it was here that she made her home. Eight Christian Thai families, connected with the American Presbyterian Mission, lived in Prao, and the welcome they gave her was heart-warming. As far as they were concerned they wished she would stay among them all the time, teaching them in her rather faltering Thai, leading English Bible classes, tending their physical ills. But her call was to the Lisu, and those simple-hearted Thai believers respected it.

'Mr. Boon Tiang had likened my search for the Lisu to the Shepherd seeking the lost sheep, who could not rest until He found them,' she wrote after one of her long, hard journeys into the hills. 'So as we climbed the steep mountain ridges, slipping on the stones, hot, panting and thirsty, I felt the Heavenly Presence had gone before, and He had bleeding feet. How near He was as we trudged along, as it seemed, in His footsteps.'

For a few of those long journeys she had Dorothy's companionship, but not for many. The younger worker was taken ill and at the height of the rainy season had to be escorted over miles of muddy paths to the high road where the jeep that was to take her to the hospital in Chiengmai was waiting.

Lilian wrote,

> I do not know whether Dorothy will be able to return here. Mr. Carlson thought it most unlikely. I had determined before coming back this term that I would not spend another term in the mountains alone. However, the Lord has been speaking to me about this. If it is His will, then I can do it. 'I can do all things through Christ which strengtheneth me.'

And the sturdy little figure waved goodbye as the jeep drew off, then turned to trudge back along the narrow, slippery paths between the rice fields, alone.

Perhaps it was inevitable that it would be so. 'Lilian is a loner,' her fellow missionaries agreed between themselves sometimes, as they saw her taking, quite unconsciously, an individual line, or sticking determinedly to her own ideas about how things ought to be done. Very few had her physical stamina, or her ability to put up for long periods with poor food, lack of privacy and hard living conditions. She had ploughed a lonely furrow for so long that mealtimes and prearranged schedules were airily ignored if they interfered with what she was doing. The very qualities that made her such a successful pioneer among the tribes were those that made her a fellow worker rather difficult to live with.

Lilian was forty-three years old when she faced the

probability that for the remainder of her missionary life among the Lisu she would be alone. She knew there was no one else to take Dorothy's place. The north Thailand team was undermanned as it was, and there were other tribes to be reached—the Yao, the Shan, the Akha the Pwo Karen, the Miao . . .

Facing afresh the solitude she knew so well was to her the taking up of the cross in a more definite and personal way. The thought of the Cross of Christ, and what it had meant to Him came out time and time again in her letters now.

Those of us who are God's messengers must have the cross at the centre of our lives. We must be willing to die that life may come out of death. 'That Jesus person is coming,' called the children as I approached a Lisu home. May God make me ready to die always that Christ may live in me, making me 'a Jesus person' indeed.

> O mark Thy holy Cross
> On motive, preference, on all fond desire
> On that which doth in any form aspire
> Set Thou that sign of loss.

She made frequent visits to Lisu villages during the following months, always optimistic at the slightest sign of friendliness although there were times when hospitality failed and she had to spread out her bed bag to sleep alone in an empty granary, a 'haunted house', or an old discarded chicken pen. Patience and persistence were eventually rewarded. Suspicion was broken down as her medical treatment proved effective and again she was asked to come and live among them.

Again she went. Retaining the little teakwood house in Prao as a base, she set off one day in February in spite of the pleas of the serving woman left in charge:

'Don't go! Stay here. There are thieves up there. A

foreigner has just been killed by robbers on Elephant Mountain.'

'I know,' replied Lilian. She had heard about the American engineer who had been killed near Chiengrai a few weeks previously. 'But I'm a missionary, and I must be willing to sacrifice, even give my life if necessary, so that the Lisu may hear of the Saviour.' So she set off, accompanied by two Thai carriers from whose bamboo poles dangled boxes and baskets, a table and a wicker chair. Through the shady forest, across streams, up the mountainside they went until at last they reached the summit from which Lilian could see on the opposite ridge a small yellow bamboo shack surrounded by a fence to keep out the pigs and cows, the horses and chickens, and knew that that was her home.

'Have you come alone?' So ask the Lisu men and women and the Thai, too. They cannot conceive how I can climb the mountains alone, live alone, work alone. In the East people go everywhere in twos or in larger groups. It seems strange to them for anyone, especially a woman, to be any length of time alone. I was reading the other day and these words came to me, 'They two went on . . .' and I realized as I read that it was true, Christ and I, because Christ indwells. 'They two went on . . .' But I must confess that I am sometimes tempted to turn back instead of going on."

The temptation to give up was one that evidently assailed her very powerfully during those last few months of her life. Not that she or anyone else suspected that the end was so near, that the lonely pilgrimage was nearly over. She was in good health, the countryside was no more disturbed than usual, and in any case although the witch doctors opposed her she had no personal enemies. There was less likelihood of death by accident or violence there on the quiet mountainside than on the motorized highways or in the crowded cities. The conflict she found herself shrinking

155

from was that waged in the spiritual, not the physical realm. One of the last letters she wrote ended with the quotation,

> My hand is on the plough, my faltering hand
> But all in front of me is untilled land.
> The wilderness and the solitary place,
> The lonely desert with its interspace.
>   . . . My courage is outworn,
> Keep me from turning back.
> The handles of my plough with tears are wet,
> The shears with rust are spoiled, and yet, and yet,
> My God! My God! Keep me from turning back.

But the long vista of lonely years ahead proved to be only a gloomy mirage after all.

Instead, by one of the inexplicable acts of man's wickedness she was translated for ever into the presence of her Lord, where the cares and trials of her earthly life would be

>   . . . in memory's sunset air
> Like mountain ranges overpast
> In purple distance fair.

One Saturday in April 1959 she set off early to go down to her base in Prao on one of her periodical visits to collect her mail and replenish her stores of food and medicine. Two Thai carriers, a Lisu and a Chinese were also travelling down to the plain that day, and she joined them for the journey through the jungle to the bottom of the mountain, where the two Thai carriers stopped at an inn for a smoke of opium, while the Lisu and the Chinese went on. Lilian rested for a while, then decided to go on ahead of the carriers. She was a slow walker, rather unsteady on her feet, and she knew they would soon catch her up, so with her bamboo staff and her shoulder bag, and her big hat on the back of her head, she started off alone. . . .

A few hours later the British Consul in north Thailand received word that an Englishwoman had been found murdered on a lonely trail on the way to Prao. She was identified as Lilian Hamer of the C.I.M. Overseas Missionary Fellowship. She had been shot at fairly close range by an unknown assailant using a sawn-off shotgun, and had been found dead crouching over in an attitude of prayer by the side of the path leading through a copse. There was no evident motive for the attack,*

So the bald facts appear to man. But on the day before Lilian moved from her little teakwood house in Prao to live among the Lisu in the shack on the mountains she read a verse which came to her with a strange significance. 'Behold, I send an Angel before thee to keep thee in the way, and to bring thee into the place which I have prepared.' She thought at the time it referred to the shack on the mountains, but that, after all, was only a stop on the way.

*   *   *

The news of Lilian Hamer's death brought a shock of dismay and horror through the whole of the North Thailand field, and far beyond. She was the first member of the missionary fellowship to be murdered since the withdrawal from China, and her death highlighted afresh the dangers inherent in obeying the Master's command to carry the Good News into all the world. Memorial services were held, plaques with her name inscribed appeared on walls, a book was written about her. With the passing of the years, and the death by violence of others in the Overseas Missionary Fellowship overshadowing her own, those few brief hours when she was dying alone by the side of the trail can be seen

* Years later it emerged that an opium addict was the culprit. He had accepted a bribe from a witch doctor and a Chinese quack who saw they were losing their power over the people because of Lilian's medical and spiritual work. A Lisu church now stands within 100 yards of the tree under which she was killed.

in perspective as only the crowning sacrifice of her life of dogged determination to stick to her post, come what may. It was the life she lived, even more than the death she died, that makes her a worthy representative of the women who have endured the privations and braved the dangers of pioneer work to carry the gospel of Christ among the tribes of south-east Asia.